From Wentworth to the Western Front:

The World War One Odyssey of Private John Warns

Rich Lofthus

Lulu Publishing Services rev. date: 09/17/2018

CONTENTS

PREFACE

From Wentworth to the Western Front: The World War One Odyssey of Private John Warns is structured around the World War One correspondence of the John Warns family and seeks to place that correspondence into the wider context of the World War One era. In nearly all instances the letters appear in the narrative in the chronological order in which they were written and received. In the spirit of trying to preserve the voice of those who wrote the letters, the authentic spelling and grammar has been preserved, with a few exceptions in which the author determined that slight corrections were required to enhance the reader's ability to understand what the original writers intended to convey.

ACKNOWLEDGEMENTS

I would like to thank the late Marvin and Leona Warns, son and daughter-in-law of John Warns, for their dedication to keeping the memory of John Warns alive by collecting and preserving the letters and other materials referred to in this book. In 2003, fifty-one years after the death of John Warns (1952), they decided that although John Warns had labeled the Warns family correspondence as "private, not for public viewing", enough years had passed, and it was time to tell this World War One story. Marvin and Leona then entrusted me with the awesome privilege of access to a goldmine of primary sources that they had faithfully collected and preserved over several decades. In 2006 an article entitled *"Over Here, Over There: The World War One Correspondence of the Private John Warns Family"* was published in the journal entitled *South Dakota History.* In the ensuing years, the Warns family continued to release items they had collected, and in 2009, Lloyd Schoenefeld, son of John's sister Anna Warns, contributed numerous letters that John Warns wrote to his sister Anna. On numerous occasions Marvin and Leona met me in towns across the upper Midwest (Fargo, North Dakota, Inwood, Iowa, Mobridge, Aberdeen, Britton, Sioux Falls, Wentworth, Pierre and Yankton, South Dakota) and supplemented my South Dakota Humanities Speaker's Bureau presentations of this story with displays of John Warns' World War One memorabilia. At one of the presentations in Sioux Falls in 2012, Marvin Warns informed me that he was ill and would no longer be able to make these trips. Marvin passed away in 2012 and Leona passed away in 2018, and I regret that they are unable to witness the completion of this project. I want to thank my colleague, Jason Heron, for his constructive comments and editing of the manuscript. I would also like to thank various student assistants who contributed to this project: Crystal Miller, Mandy (Carlson) Hanson, and especially Michaela Ramm, who worked closely with me as we integrated numerous letters into the narrative in 2014. Her interest and encouragement inspired me to carry on, and her direct assistance proved that four eyes are better than two when it comes to reading early twentieth-century handwriting. Thanks also to former students Caitlyn Oien and Samantha (Blake) Lindholm, who made the supreme "sacrifice" of missing a day of classes and supported me by attending a presentation based on this story at the 2014 Dakota Conference in Sioux Falls, South Dakota.

Rich Lofthus

August 3, 2018
Yankton, South Dakota

CHAPTER ONE

Explosion

"I am inclined to think that Sherman slandered
hell when he compared it to war."
- Gil

After a would-be assassin's bomb was deflected off their car and wounded someone in another car, Archduke Franz Ferdinand and his consort Sophie had to wonder what was around every corner as their motorcade maneuvered through the streets of Sarajevo on 28 June, 1914. Undeterred, Archduke Ferdinand visited the town hall and spoke at a reception. Back on the streets of Sarajevo, as the motorcade paused to re-direct at 10:30 A. M., the Archduke's car was motionless just five feet from Serbian nationalist Garvilo Princip. Princip fired two shots, hitting the Archduke's jugular with one and the abdomen of the Duchess with the other. By 11:00 A. M. the future King of Austria-Hungary and his wife were dead.[1] In the tumultuous summer of 1914, the Archduke's assassination plunged the continent of Europe into one of the most destructive wars of all time. The Central Powers of Germany and Austria-Hungary engaged the Allied powers of Great Britain, France and Russia in what would become a long, indecisive struggle featuring trench warfare and stalemate. President Woodrow Wilson was well aware that the United States had recently experienced a massive influx of immigrants, whose ties to the various European countries created a confusing patchwork of divided loyalties.[2] Consequently he proclaimed that the United States would remain a neutral power. Over five-thousand miles away from the catastrophic events in Europe, the family of Peter and Dora Warns had established a farm and family in rural Wentworth, South Dakota. As German-Americans they were members of the largest (8.3 million) and "most affluent immigrant group in the United States," a group that, according to a 1908 survey, was ranked as the "most admirable."[3] As World War I entered its initial stages, these German-American residents of one of the most isolationist locations in the United States could not have anticipated that one day the United States would declare war on Germany in a turn of events that would dramatically impact their family.

Each side of the Peter and Dora Warns family was deeply connected to Germany. The Warns side of their family included Peter's father, Diedrich Jacob Warns, who was born in 1825 in Reepsholt Ostfriesland, Germany. Diedrich Jacob Warns immigrated to the United States in 1846. After serving as a Lutheran pastor in Illinois and Indiana, Jacob Warns and his wife Maria Gruber Warns, along with their sons Jacob and Peter (who was born in Holland, Indiana in 1868 and later became John Warns' father) moved to Wentworth, Dakota Territory in 1885 and established a homestead of one-hundred and sixty acres.[4]

The Unzelman side of the Peter and Dora Warns family included Dorothea's father John, who was born in Germany in 1827, and Dorothea's mother Sophie Bartles, who was born in Germany in 1840. John Unzelman and Sophie met in Wisconsin and were married in 1856, and Dorothea was one of their fifteen children. In 1878 John and Sophie Unzelman moved from Wisconsin to Dakota Territory and established a farm six and three-fourths miles northeast of Wentworth. In 1883 they were founding members of a German Lutheran Church, located in rural Rutland Township.[5] Their daughter, Sophie Dorothea (Dora) Unzelman married Peter Warns in Wentworth on 25 October, 1893. Peter and Dora Warns established a farm three miles north of Wentworth. As part of their farming operation, the Warns family raised swine and sold baby chicks to surrounding towns and counties.[6] Their family included seven children: John, the oldest, who was born in 1895; Martha and Martin, born in 1896; Anna (nicknamed Tom or Tommy), born in 1900; Walter, born in 1903;

Dorothea (nicknamed Dimples), born in 1906; and Selma (Sally), born in 1909.[7] They were all active members of Saint Peter's Lutheran Church in Wentworth, which sponsored a parochial school, and featured worship services conducted in the German language.

In the spring of 1917 the United States entered the war on the side of the Allied powers. The American public was asked to abandon neutrality and ethnic loyalties to the Central Powers, in favor of complete support for the American war effort against the Germans who were now portrayed in official United States government propaganda as barbaric Huns.[8] While the United States had previously waged wars of expansion and become an imperial power in control of areas such as the Philippine and Hawaiian Islands, until its entry into World War One the United States had served as a form of promised land for immigrants. But when the United States interjected itself into World War One, a dramatic transformation from neutrality to a wartime America took place, and in that process the United States became a crusading state, waging war to extend its democratic ideals, establishing an ideological justification for going to war that has characterized many subsequent wars, including the failed attempt to maintain a non-Communist South Vietnam and the problematic invasion of Iraq in 2003.

John Warns, the eldest son of Peter and Dora Warns, was drafted into the army in April, 1918, and served with the Eighty-ninth Division on the Western Front. Various members of his family and the community of Wentworth, South Dakota corresponded with John during his basic training in Funston, Kansas, his time in England, his active duty on the Western Front, his service in the army of occupation that entered Germany in 1919, and while he was returning home to South Dakota. In response, John's letters provide a rich narrative from each of these locations. The wartime correspondence of the Warns family from Wentworth, South Dakota spans the years 1915-1919, includes hundreds of letters, and when combined with other items from the period collected and preserved by the Warns family, and placed within the historical context of that time, provides us an opportunity to more fully understand one of the most dramatic turning points in United States history through the eyes of a South Dakota family.[9]

A variety of themes emerge from the Warns family correspondence: it reveals the manner in which rural South Dakota was drawn, as never before, directly into these cataclysmic world-wide events, it also demonstrates that the propaganda efforts of the Wilson administration, in its relentless drive to create monolithic support for the war, created an atmosphere in which intolerance became a "virtue", and as a result, controversy appeared in Wentworth when so-called "slackers" questioned the war effort and farmers challenged the political status quo by attempting to join the Nonpartisan League. The lengthy letters, often over ten pages, also express the strong bonds of faith and family, especially between John Warns and his mother Dora and sister Anna, which nurtured and sustained those on the home and war fronts. It also reflects the ingredients that contributed to Private Warns' survival on the Western Front: some good luck, reliance on his Christian faith, and some assistance from Velvet smoking tobacco and fine German wines. We also learn that long after World War One, John Warns achieved a sense of reconciliation with his former foes. He completed an odyssey that originated with his draft in 1918, when, in 1947, he renewed his acquaintance with a German family he had met during the 1919 American occupation of Germany.

In 1915 John Warns was a twenty-year-old grandson of a German immigrant who worked on the family farm near Wentworth, South Dakota, delivered mail part-time with a horse and buggy, and avidly collected stamps. The level of his interest in stamp collecting is reflected in the fact that he was chairman of the Dakota Philatelic Association, and had compiled its annual yearbook in 1914.[10] The first letter of this remarkable collection of correspondence and documents is from a stamp-collecting friend named Gil of Grand Forks, North Dakota. Gil was writing to tell John why he had not heard from him in a while, and he explained that when the war started in 1914 his uncle, Ernst van Mackenstadt, who was an officer in the German army, invited Gil to join him on the Western Front. Eager to experience the thrill of war on a first-hand basis, Gil remarked, "needless to say, I went." Gil offered this reflection on his wartime experiences:

> I went over there for the experience and also for the excitement. I got enough experience to satisfy me and more than enough excitement... War is all right in a way but having seen some of it I am inclined to think that

> Sherman slandered hell when he compared it with war.
> I am inclined to think that the devil would blush with
> shame to do some of the things that are perpetrated in the
> name of war. I never, in my worst imagining, pictured war
> as bad as it really is.[11]

Gil arrived in Bremen on 14 September, 1914 "going via Denmark, across the Kiel Canal at Kiel, thence to Lubeck and Bremen."[12] Germany's strategy included going through neutral Belgium in order to invade France, which brought Great Britain into the war. As elements of the Belgium population resisted the German invasion, British propaganda claimed the German army retaliated by committing various atrocities along the way. Gil clearly offered a different perspective, and as he joined his uncle's regiment at Brussels he remarked, "I didn't fully realize what war was until I got into Belgium. Poor country. A simple, rather conceited people, misled and misruled into entering into a war which they could just as well have missed." Gil viewed the Great War as an opportunity for Germany to check British imperialism and create an opportunity for Germany to expand its sphere of influence. He confidently predicted that the Germans would win the war, observing that "probably it is for the best as when the war is over Great Britain will have lost her control over the rest of the world and other nations will have a chance to peacefully grow and develop."[13] Gil's sympathy for the German cause was most clear when he wrote, "while in Brussels I had my first view of Kaiser Wilhelm and no German can look in his eyes and not absorb some of his enthusiasm, some of his patriotism, and some of his love for, and faith in Germany." Later in his letter, Gil described Kaiser Wilhelm as "a medium sized man with a fire in his eyes that burns right through you. The points of his famous mustache have been clipped so that he don't look quite so war like but that don't affect his war spirit any."[14] Gil explained his duties as follows: "I was connected with the telegraph and signal corps for six weeks or until we reached Dixmude. I didn't get into any real battle until about the first of November."[15]

Gil and the Germans crossed the Yser River on 23 October, 1914, and he observed that, "From that point on it was one continuous roar. The 25th saw some pretty heavy fighting with the Belgium's yielding, and all I could do was to pound a telegraph instrument while the rest were doing the fighting. When there is so much fight in the air a fellow just aches to get into it." Gil's most direct experience with the horrors of war came on 26 October, 1914:

> The next day I guess the English must have arrived for a terrific stand was made against us and then the bloomin' fish opened the dikes and flooded us out. We dropped back as fast as we could but thousands of dead and wounded were flooded over. Then began what is probably the queerest battle in history. On the 31st I again interviewed my uncle and as a result shouldered my rifle and joined my cousin's company of infantry… I am enclosing a sketch of the operation I took part in and by looking at that you may be able to follow me better.[16]

Later in the same skirmish, Gil informed John, "we had been fighting continuously for fifty hours without sleep and very little food but nevertheless our company was ordered out to hold the river dike until what was left of our regiment could fall back to the trenches. Believe me, Warns, I have been good and tired more than once but I never knew what it was to be completely exhausted until then, and there we were expected to resist an attack by a superior force of fairly fresh troops." After a brief interlude, the English "thinking we were completely routed, charged and then our clickers got busy and let loose with the most murderous cross fire I ever saw. The English started down the incline but as that was narrow we got them as fast as they came while up on the dikes our machine guns were simply mowing them down like windrows. The dead and the wounded were massed up in a conglomerate heap of mangled bodies and blood. The moans and screams were simply awful. And then to cap the climax the battery across the river got the range and dropped shell after shell into that seething mass of what was once humanity."[17] Given the enormous loss of life, Gil was moved to question English strategy; "I have often wondered if the English officers were crazy to order their men into a trap like that. Finally, the guns stopped, and we jumped for the rear of our trenches with fixed bayonets and got what was left of the charge as they came over the trench. It's hard to think about such waste of life especially of such men as they—for they did know how to die."[18] The First Battle of Ypres is now considered to have officially ended on 22 November, 1915.[19] As Gil's graphic first-hand description of a small portion of that battle reveals, 1915 ended with a startling preview of the kind of carnage that would come to characterize World War I. At the outset of World War I it is certain that many Americans of German ancestry supported their homeland and hoped that the Central Powers would win the war. Few, if any, acted on the basis of those sentiments as enthusiastically as Gil. Gil's pro-German stance and his attempt to claim that the sufferings of the Belgium people were really self-inflicted ran counter to the findings of American war correspondent Richard Harding Davis. Davis openly questioned President Wilson's policy of neutrality in late 1914 when, after spending several months on the Western Front, he wrote, "Were the conflict in Europe a fair fight, the duty of every American would be to keep on the side-lines and preserve an open mind. But it is not a fair fight." After witnessing the gruesome manner in which the Germans destroyed the Belgium city of Louvain, Richard Harding Davis observed, "To destroy cathedrals is not a fair fight. That is the way Germany is fighting. She is defying the rules of war and the rules of humanity . . . . When a mad dog runs amok in a village it is the duty of every farmer to get his gun and destroy it, not to lock himself indoors and toward the dog and men who face him preserve a neutral mind."[20] American novelist Edith Wharton spent seven months on the Western Front in 1915 and her assessment of the situation lined up with Davis, rather than Gil. Wharton wrote "describing the huge tiger slashes that the German beast flung over the land" and attempted to convince her readers that "the atrocities one hears about are true, I know of many alas, too well authenticated." She also expressed doubts regarding the wisdom of neutrality when she proclaimed, "it should be known that it is in America's interest to stem the flow of this hideous savagery, by opinion if not be by action. No civilized race can remain neutral in feeling now."[21]

With awareness of the growing tensions between the United States and Germany, Gil concluded by asking John Warns to keep quiet about his adventures because he was seeking employment with the postal service in Grand Forks.[22] Since no known response to this letter has survived, we do not know if or how John Warns responded, or if he shared any of his friend's support for the German cause. Gil's letter had most certainly presented John with a lively introduction to the war from the German perspective. Gil's fascination with war had been dampened by his front-line odyssey and he was glad to be "back in the good old United States again." He told Warns that "if the Statue of Liberty wants to see me again she will have to turn around and face west."[23] As the relationship between the United States and Germany continued to deteriorate, John Warns must have wondered: would he have an opportunity to gaze upon the Statue of Liberty?

CHAPTER TWO

Over Here

"The world must be made safe for democracy."
-Woodrow Wilson

A s the war years dragged on, support for the Allied cause grew steadily in the United States. When America's neutrality eventually collapsed in April of 1917, entry into the war was accompanied by Wilson's monolithic demand for a unified home front, which had the unfortunate consequence of making intolerance an American virtue. The community of Wentworth, South Dakota and the Warns family were drawn into controversy when attempts to organize the Nonpartisan League in South Dakota were met with strident opposition from South Dakota's established political parties, Governor Peter Norbeck and former President Theodore Roosevelt. A major factor that contributed to the collapse of neutrality was a torpedo attack by a German submarine on the British ocean-liner Lusitania on 7 May, 1915. Of the more than one thousand persons who perished in the incident, one hundred and twenty-eight were American.[24] In negotiations after this tragedy, Germany promised to practice restricted submarine warfare. American neutrality was strained once again when, in February of 1917, the Wilson administration was made aware of what came to be called the "Zimmerman Note." In this message German Foreign Minister Dr. Alfred von Zimmerman stated that if a return to unrestricted submarine warfare brought the United States into the war, Mexico was invited to wage war with Germany against the United States. Mexico's reward would be to regain Texas, New Mexico and Arizona.[25] In an attempt to mount an offensive the Germans knew might bring the United States into the war, Germany broke its 1915 pledge in the spring of 1917, and soon American ships were the targets of Germany's return to the policy of unrestricted submarine warfare. President Woodrow Wilson sensed that the American people could not be genuinely motivated to go to war unless the rationale for going to war and the intended consequences of the engagement resonated with commonly held ideals. On 2 April, 1917 President Wilson asked for a congressional declaration of war as he made an emotional appeal to the idealism of the American people, attempting to recast the war as an ideological conflict: "Neutrality is no longer feasible or desirable where the peace of the world is involved and the freedom of its peoples, and the menace to that peace and freedom lies in the existence of autocratic governments, backed by organized force which is controlled wholly by their will, not by the will of the people."[26] Wilson envisioned a world in which democratic government was the key to world peace when he stated that "a steadfast concert for peace can never be maintained except by a partnership of democratic nations."[27] His speech concluded with a rhetorical flourish in which he displayed his "ability to tap the latent idealism in the soul of many Americans."[28] Wilson claimed that the United States should enter the war "to fight thus for the ultimate peace of the world and for the liberation of its peoples, the German peoples included; for the rights of nations, great and small, and the privilege of men everywhere to choose their way of life and of obedience."[29] Wilson's boldest statement was that "the world must be made safe for democracy."[30] Wilson biographer A. Scott Berg commented on the significance of Wilson's speech by observing that, "It is what I consider the greatest foreign policy speech in American history, because imbedded within this speech is a single sentence, which for the last hundred years, has been the bedrock of all American foreign policy. And that sentence is quite simply this: "The world must be made safe for democracy."[31] Wilson was well aware that a toxic brew of ancient causes such as imperialism, nationalism and militarism were the long-term causes of the war. He was also cognizant of the fact that the more immediate causes were assassinations and the indiscriminate sinking of ocean liners. But Wilson was also a staunch idealist, convinced that these same long term and immediate causes would serve as a seething cauldron for future conflicts unless a new world order was established. For Wilson, World War I represented an opportunity to create this new world order in which war would no longer be used to settle differences—a new world order predicated on self-determination and democracy, and American entry into the war was essential to the realization of his vision. Historian David Kennedy emphasizes the continuity between Wilson's reputation as a leader of the Progressive Movement and his request that the United States enter World War I:

> That so many thoughtful men and women passed so swiftly from favoring peace to embracing war testifies less to the weakness of their convictions than to the deep-running consistency of the progressive mentality, able to find grounds for hopeful affirmation even in the face of unprecedented calamity. It testified equally strongly to Wilson's remarkable adroitness at figuring the war in terms congenial to the American mind, and particularly appealing to progressives: a war for democracy, a war to end war, a war to protect liberalism, a war against militarism, a war to redeem barbarous Europe, a crusade.[32]

The Senate debated Wilson's request for a war declaration on 4 April, 1917. Between 4:00 P. M. and 6:45 P. M. Senator Robert La Follette delivered an impassioned anti-war speech, offering a critique of Wilson's request for a declaration of war before he became one of just six Senators (82-6) who voted not to go to war. Despite the consensus for going to war, "not a hand clapped, not a voice cheered." The debate in the House got underway on 5 April and spilled over into the early morning hours of 6 April. Representative Janette Rankin of Montana, casting the initial vote of her career, was one of fifty House members (373-50) to vote against going to war. President Wilson signed the declaration of war on 6 April, 1917. The United States entered the Great War on Good Friday.[33]

On 4 April, 1917, by order of President Wilson, the Committee on Public Information (CPI) was created to propagate Wilson's ideological version of World War I.[34] Before long the CPI, with George Creel as Chairman, had produced a thirty-two page "Official Bulletin" that was distributed to virtually every newspaper in the United States.[35] Creel understood that his goal was to create the "war will" that in a democracy could only come about when all the people "concentrate and consecrate body and soul and spirit in a supreme effort of spirit and sacrifice." This would require a "passionate belief in the justice of America's cause," that once achieved would "meld the people of the United States into one white hot mass instinct with fraternity, devotion, courage and deathless determination."[36] Along with Wilson's CPI, Congress generated its own avalanche of patriotism in the form of acts that were designed to suppress opposition by criminalizing dissent. In June, 1917 the Espionage Act made it a crime to "aid the enemy" or "obstruct the United States war effort." In May, 1918 the Sedition Act declared it illegal to "utter, print, write, or publish, any disloyal, profane, scurrilous, or abusive language about the government, Constitution, or armed forces." "Furthermore, "saying anything" to discourage the purchase of war bonds was declared to be criminal activity.[37] It was clear that the Wilson administration and Congress determined to wage the war with a united home front, as the CPI, and the Espionage and Sedition Acts represented a heavy-handed near closure of free speech in the United States, and the end result was that "America entered a period of regression as egregious as any in American history."[38] When American Socialist Eugene Debs was charged with violation of the Espionage Act in 1918 on the grounds that he had obstructed military recruitment, and his case came before the Supreme Court, the Court referred to *Schenck v. United States*, in which Justice Oliver Wendell Holmes, Jr. wrote, "When a nation is at war many things that might be said in time of peace are such a hindrance to its efforts that their utterance will not be endured so long as men fight and that no Court could regard them as protected by any constitutional right." Debs was sentenced to ten years in prison. Commenting on Debs' case, Wilson remarked "once the Congress of the United States declared war, silence on his [Debs] part would have been the proper course to pursue."[39] With enormous irony, the campaign to make the world safe for democracy would feature the restriction of basic Constitutional rights on the home front. This monolithic demand to conform brought most Americans into the fold, but there was enough dissent to create tensions in communities such as Wentworth, South Dakota.

In the Warns family hometown, the transformation from neutrality to a wartime America was clearly supported by the local newspaper, the *Wentworth Enterprise*, whose editor did all he could to whip up the Kaiser-stomping patriotism that permeated the United States following America's entry into the conflict. One week after printing President Wilson's speech requesting a declaration of war against Germany, the *Wentworth Enterprise* published a letter "From a Patriotic German-American" on its front page. Jacob Cratts, the author of the letter, provides a testimonial as to why he came to America from Germany:

> When I landed in this country I secured work at once and received more money for one month's work than I got in Germany for one year's work. I sent for my folks and I am proud that they are all true American citizens and will answer the president's call to arms against Germany or any other country when needed. Referring to the pro-German sentiments of some immigrants, he continued, "I don't see how my countrymen can go back on Uncle Sam. They came here without a cent and made money here; now they want to fight the country that feeds them. The Kaiser never did anything for them or me... I hope to see the day when he is kicked out of Germany and a president put in his place... Stop all foreign papers printed in the United States. If they can't read English let them learn; keep all foreign languages out of the schools. The English language is good enough for everybody.[40]

Cratts' suggestion about eliminating all foreign languages from the schools actually anticipated what would become state-wide policy in South Dakota just over a year later, a policy that owed its origins to the determination of the Wilson administration to curtail any pro-German sympathies. In an effort to rally support for the war and eradicate pro-German sentiment, the Wilson administration created the National Council of Defense in 1917. In May, 1917 Governor Peter Norbeck, in response to a request from the National Council of Defense in Washington, appointed a State Council of Defense. The mission of the Council was "to assist in every way possible in the prosecution of the war, taking all necessary steps for the full utilization of the military, industrial, and civil resources of the state."[41] In May, 1918 a special session of the South Dakota legislature adopted policies "prohibiting instruction in any foreign language in the common schools."[42] As a follow up to this legislation, the State Council of Defense "explicitly ordered all instruction in the German language to cease, except in classes of religious instruction already organized", and issued an order "prohibiting the use of the enemy's language in public conversation and over the telephone, except in cases of extreme emergency."[43]

The entirely new and oppressive situation in which Americans of German ancestry now found themselves contrasted dramatically with their status prior to 1914, when they were "probably the most esteemed immigrant group in America, regarded as easily assimilable, upright citizens."[44] The travails of the transition these Americans faced were the subject of a letter John Warns received from Ida Rottlufs, a teacher from Oldham, South Dakota in October, 1917:

> Have joined the Red Cross. It seems to me everybody should give to that or buy a Liberty Bond for the more money we give now the less it is going to cost us in men, and surely none of us love our money more than we do our men. That's my answer on the moral question on that Red Cross article you said you were writing. You see I was very much of a Pro-German until war was declared. Since then I've done a lot of thinking and I see that while Germany has been fighting for a material reason, we are fighting for a principle—as old as the world itself—that people don't seem to understand. And the reason they don't understand is because they understand Germany's reason for fighting, because it is something transient, something for which they themselves are fighting in their everyday life. But enough of this. We don't agree anyway, so where's the use of talking? ... Do you know yet when you will go to training camp?[45]

Warns had been selected for military service and ordered to report for duty to Madison, South Dakota on 26 April, 1918. However, before he could enter the military, John Warns' patriotism was called into question in a controversy that indicates how the transition from neutrality to a wartime America was fraught with difficulties for the community of Wentworth, South Dakota.

In January of 1918, Wentworth's local weekly newspaper, the *Wentworth Enterprise*, began to detail the nature of a controversy in which the patriotism of several Wentworth area citizens was questioned due to their membership in a political organization known as the Nonpartisan League (NPL). The NPL was a political organization founded in western North Dakota in February and March, 1915 by Albert E. Bowen Jr. and Arthur C. Townley, each of whom had previously been affiliated with the Socialist Party.[46] As an organization the NPL claimed that neither of the two major political parties truly represented the concerns of farmers, and it called for state-owned mills, elevators and banks as a way for farmers to curtail the power of corporations in Minneapolis and Chicago that were mismanaging their economic well-being. Instead of following the Populist model of forming a doomed-to-fail third party, the NPL constructed a set of demands and then endorsed candidates from either party who agreed to support their agenda. The NPL strategy produced a political revolution in the 1916 North Dakota elections as the NPL took control of the state's Republican Party and elected a Leaguer named Lynn Frazier as governor. Soon the NPL looked outside of North Dakota in an attempt to galvanize farmers into one large voting bloc.[47] Records demonstrate that John Warns joined The Farmers Nonpartisan League of South Dakota on 25 January, 1918.[48]

Governor Peter Norbeck faced re-election in 1918, and as he observed the NPL's attraction to many South Dakota farmers, he designed a strategy to undermine the appeal of the NPL. Norbeck's approach included contrasting his achievements with the failures of the NPL in North Dakota, support of constitutional amendments that would allow additional "state enterprises," and denunciation of the League leaders "as being radical Socialists and disloyal in the war."[49] When charging the NPL with disloyalty, Norbeck was following the lead of former Republican President Theodore Roosevelt. In a *Kansas City Star* editorial on October 1, 1917, Roosevelt employed his pen and prestige in an attempt to portray the

Nonpartisan League as the "Nonpatriotic" League. Commenting on a September, 1917 NPL rally in Saint Paul, Minnesota, Roosevelt opined, "Ten days ago a ghost dance was held in St. Paul under the auspices of the Non-Partisan League, with Senator La Follette as the star performer." In his speech, La Follette did refer to the fact that he had voted against the April, 1917 declaration of war against Germany and he defended his right to dissent. The Associated Press misquoted La Follette's speech, suggesting he had said, "I wasn't in favor of beginning the war. We had no grievances."[50] The rest of his speech was ignored, and Roosevelt was now categorizing La Follette and anyone who would "directly or indirectly talk against our government for going to war or talk against any step which it takes for the efficient waging of the war" as a "Shadow Hun."[51]

When Norbeck attempted to link the NPL with radical Socialists, he was also following Roosevelt's lead. In a series of five *Kansas City Star* editorials that spanned from March 19, 1918 to September 12, 1918, Roosevelt made the wildly irresponsible accusation that NPL leader Arthur C. Townley was a "native Bolsheviki", he predicted that, "Utter ruin will befall this country if it falls into the hands of Haywoods and Townleys", and he called upon farmers to "repudiate the Non-Partisan League just as long as it submits to such leadership as that of most of the men who are at present at its head." Furthermore, Roosevelt claimed that spies and slackers "have received aid and cooperation, conscientiously and unconscientiously, by many evils in pacifist and Bolshevist societies and in organizations like the I. W. W. and Non-Partisan League." In these editorials, Roosevelt repeatedly claimed that he was sympathetic to the injustices that had prompted farmers to join the NPL, but he lambasted the NPL leaders— the "practical Bolsheviki in this country who are in no sense highbrows. The I. W. W. and the Non-partisan League, just as long and so far as its members submit to the dominion of leaders like Mr. Townley, represent the forces that under Lenine [Lenin] and Trotzky [Trotsky] have brought ruin to Russia, if these organizations obtained power here, they would cast this country into the same abyss with Russia." Taking direct aim at Townley, Roosevelt wrote:

> Mr. Townley's leadership in its moral purpose and na-
> tional effect entitles him to rank with Messrs. Lenine and

Trotzky, and the utterances of the League's official organ, especially in its appeals to class hatred, puts the official representatives of the League squarely in the clan with the Bolshevist leaders who have done such evil in Russia.[52]

In January 1918, the *Wentworth Enterprise* clearly endorsed former President Theodore Roosevelt's style of militant opposition to the NPL, and linked the NPL with suspected disloyalty to the World War One effort:

> Since America was forced into war with Germany and up to the present week, by keeping close tab, we have only lost eight subscribers, who could be classified as pro-German. During the past two months we have added over twenty new names of loyal Americans to our list. One German friend was frank enough to tell us that he loved the fatherland, and would not have a paper that said anything good for this country and was against the Kaiser and German militarism—so much for him, we have his number. One or two others, who were not so frank, try to hide under the cloak of the NonPartisan League, but that don't work— and we have their number, and when the proper time comes the list will be sent to the authorities.[53]

Two weeks later the *Wentworth Enterprise* published a resolution presented by Wentworth area residents who had joined the Nonpartisan League or were interested in the NPL. The resolution was a response to charges of disloyalty. On 1 February, 1918 local farmers had attempted to assemble in Wentworth to hear a NPL speaker, but the local authorities compelled them to adjourn "to the barn of a neighboring farmer" to hold the meeting. In light of these events the signers of the resolution issued a statement which, among other assertions, made the following points:

> Resolved, that we do condemn such unwarranted action on the part of the authorities who are sworn to uphold the constitution and these citizens of Wentworth who urged such action.

Whereas, the loyalty of the assembled farmers has been questioned, therefore, be it

Resolved, that inspired by the patriotic and loyal devotion to the principles of Democracy, true to the ideals of our fathers of upholding and defending human rights and human liberties, and single in our purpose to make the world safe for democracy, political and industrial, we do herby reaffirm our unalterable loyalty and allegiance to our fellow citizens and government in this worlds struggle and in their time of need, and do hereby pledge our lives, our fortunes and our sacred honor to our country and our flag in this our war…[54]

Nineteen Wentworth area residents signed the resolution, including John Warns and his father, Peter.

The *Wentworth Enterprise* published its response to the resolution in the same issue. The newspaper dismissed the resolution as "drawn up by a bunch of paid politicians and signed by a number of local farmers." It referred to the signers as those "who must resort to empty words in an attempt to prove their loyalty, instead of proving it by their deeds and actions." The critique of the resolution continues by claiming that two of the signers refused to join the Red Cross and poses this question: "Does the dollar they were asked to contribute to the Red Cross mean more to them than their 'lives' their 'fortunes' and their 'sacred honor'?" In the campaign for the sale of Liberty Bonds to fund the war, a "Blue Card" was used to gather information about individuals who refused to buy bonds. In an effort to bolster its anti-NPL stance, the *Wentworth Enterprise* brazenly published the contents of the "Blue Card" that contained information gathered about L. J. Duncan, the South Dakota Secretary of the Non-Partisan League. In response to the questions "did he buy any of last bonds? If so how many?" Duncan's response was recorded as "none". And when asked "reasons does not buy" the Liberty Bond committee reported that he:

said [he] had other debts of more importance to meet. Refused to allow employees in the office to be solicited and when one of the committee attempted to solicit one of the employees he interfered and said it was criminal for the Government to try to get money from people who had to work for a living.[55]

The *Wentworth Enterprise* went on to contend that the photographic reproduction of the Blue Card "portrays much more forcibly than the writer can illustrate, the attitude of this non-partisan leaguer toward the successful prosecution of this war" and then resorted to guilt-by-association; "the three men who last Friday attempted to hold a Non-Partisan League meeting in Wentworth are in the employ of this man Duncan", and "the principles which he advocates and stands for must necessarily be the principles which his employees are required to preach and advocate." Finally, the local newspaper expressed its solidarity with the Wilson administration's argument that freedom of assembly and freedom of speech should be put on hold until the end of World War One:

> There are of course a few signers to this resolution who speak the English language only, but the majority of the signers use the German tongue exclusively in their homes, in their religious services, and insist on being educated in German, and speak broken English despite a lifetime residence in America. This is the only class of people in the United States today who are yelling for "free speech and free assemblage." That they can do without, until the close of the war at least, the enjoyment of a few "ideals" which their "fathers" so nobly "upheld" and "defended," is the opinion of this paper.[56]

This same 7 February, 1918 edition of the *Wentworth Enterprise* reported that the NPL meeting of February 1 was forced to move out to George Bruns' farm, and that the NPL was not allowed to meet in Madison by order of the mayor. When Governor Norbeck was informed that the NPL was denied the right to meet in Madison he issued a statement claiming that "no political organization should be interfered with. It has the right to hold public meetings. None should be prevented except such as are held for the purpose of embarrassing the government in the prosecution of the war."[57] Norbeck's biographer Gilbert Fite points out that despite this statement, "Many League organizers were roughly handled, while others were barred from speaking in certain localities."[58] And Michael Lansing has discovered that Norbeck privately remarked that "these Non-partisan fellows do so much lying that they need to be stopped."[59] When A. C. Townley, the founder and National President of the NPL, and Mark Pomeroy Bates, Norbeck's 1918 opponent for governor attempted to speak in Britton, South Dakota "they were escorted out of town and as far as the state line under threat of physical violence."[60] Persecution of NPL members in the region surrounding Madison, South Dakota was sometimes directed by mob violence. Emil Sudan, an NPL organizer who farmed southwest of Mitchell, South Dakota was tarred and feathered, and then, otherwise naked, dragged behind a wagon for miles.

In nearby Minnesota, John F. McGee of the Minnesota Commission of Public Safety "viewed the Nonpartisan League as radicals trying to topple America's power structure—just like the Bolsheviks had done to the tsar in Russia." Testifying before the Senate Committee on Military Affairs on 19 April, 1918, McGee proclaimed, "A Non-Partisan Leaguer lecturer is a traitor every time. Where we made our mistake was in not establishing a firing squad in the first days of the war. We should now get busy and have that firing squad working overtime. Wait until the long casualty lists begin to come in and the Minnesota woods will not be dense enough to hide the traitors who will meet punishment for their crimes." He predicted that firing squads would have "a most-restraining influence on the disloyal, seditious and traitorous."[61] When residents of New Ulm, Minnesota assembled to request that German American soldiers not be sent to fight directly against Germans, McGee suggested that anyone who interfered with the draft "will be looking through the barbed fences of an internment camp on the prairie somewhere."[62] In June 1918 the Mayor and Marshal of Luverne, Minnesota did not go as far as McGee suggested, but they did organize a "loyalist mob" which proceeded to order NPL members to register and renounce their League membership. John Meints refused to comply and was escorted by the "loyalist mob" to the Iowa border and told never to return. When Meints returned to help his sons with the harvest he was tarred and feathered and exiled to South Dakota. Meints sued his abductors in federal court, and a jury acquitted them. When the accused returned to Luverne they were welcomed home with a brass band.[63]

In open defiance of McGee and the Minnesota Commission of Public Safety, Irene Thompson, John Warns' friend from Vergas, Minnesota, expressed her NPL solidarity:

> I am glad you are studying to be an organizer and I wish you all kinds of success in your work. My father has been organizing in this state for some time. He has fairly good luck and has put many a nail in the coffin of "Big Biz." If they will accept girls I shall try my luck also as there isn't anything I would rather do. Minnesota is slowing (slowly) coming out of the kinks and there will be quite a time here next election. We are looking forward to the fun.[64]

Eleven days later Irene wrote "it's too bad you can't organize for the League. They need men and badly too." She was disturbed by news from the war front, "I read today the Germans captured 25,000 soldiers and are hard after Paris. What will happen next?" She empathized with those suffering: "It makes one sick just to think of the fine boys that are being killed, the people starving and others dying of broken hearts." Irene was hopeful that "surely this will be the last," and hoped that the kind of political will that embodied the NPL would permeate more of society as she predicted that "People will wake up as the farmers are doing now."[65]

As President Wilson orchestrated United States entry into World War One, the transition from neutrality to war integrated rural South Dakota and the upper Midwest, a traditionally isolated rural area, into the vortex of world events *for the first time*. In particular, the community of Wentworth and the Warns family became embroiled in controversy when the attempt to organize the Nonpartisan League clashed with the attempt to curtail civil liberties that characterized the Wilson administration's drive to create monolithic support for the war on the home front. A drive to which Governor Norbeck, former President Theodore Roosevelt, and the *Wentworth Enterprise* supplied acquiescence. In a volatile wartime atmosphere Norbeck, following former President Theodore Roosevelt's lead, denounced the NPL as unpatriotic, fanning the flames of hyper-nationalism; when the constitutional rights of NPL members were blatantly violated, he conveniently jumped to the high ground to defend the right of peaceable assembly. Norbeck then looked the other way while little was done to insure that his opponents could mount an opposition. Norbeck's strategy to diminish the influence of the Nonpartisan League in South Dakota was a crafty political move as he was re-elected by a two-to-one margin on 5 November, 1918.[66] Writing as early as 1931, historian Frederick Lewis Allen offered a scathing assessment of the manner in which World War One era super patriotism smeared all opponents with the Bolshevik label:

> Innumerable other gentlemen now discovered that they could defeat whatever they wanted to defeat by tarring it conspicuously with the Bolshevist brush. Big-navy men, believers in compulsory military service, drys, anti-cigarette campaigners, anti-evolution Fundamentalists, defenders of the moral order, book censors, Jew-haters, Negro-haters, landlords, manufacturers, utility executives, upholders of every sort of cause, good, bad, and indifferent, all wrapped themselves in Old Glory and the mantle of the Founding Fathers and allied their opponents with Lenin.[67]

In his analysis of the 1919 Red Scare, Robert K. Murray also critiqued the dubious strategy of dumping all opponents in the same barrel when he pointed out that those who championed 100 per cent Americanism often made no attempt to distinguish between "democratic liberalism, evolutionary socialism, and revolutionary communism. Instead, they blindly labeled all persons who did not agree with them "Bolsheviki," and repeated their charges as often as possible. In that sense, they rapidly mastered the technique of the demagogue or dictator—achieve by repetition and exaggeration what you cannot secure by the truth."[68] The United States was now at war against Germany, and in an atmosphere fueled by government sanctioned war-time hysteria, Peter and John Warns were fluent German speakers, they attended a church in which services were conducted in

German, and they had joined a political organization, the Nonpartisan League, which presented a direct challenge to the traditional two-party system, and had been labeled disloyal by as prestigious a figure as former President Theodore Roosevelt. Their loyalty to the United States had been called into question.

CHAPTER THREE

Over There

"Love Bids Him Stay but Duty Calls to the Man in Khaki"
-Keystone View Company Stereograph, Number 77

I f anyone still had doubts about John Warns' loyalty to the United States, his compliance with the draft in April 1918 should have settled the issue. His Order of Induction notice sternly warned that "willful failure to report with an intent to evade military service constitutes desertion from the Army of the United States, which, in time of war, is a capital offense." Inductees were instructed to bring only "hand baggage", in which:

> You should take only the following articles: A pair of strong comfortable shoes to relieve your feet from your new regulation marching shoes; not to exceed four extra suits of underclothing; not to exceed six extra pairs of socks; four face and two bath towels; a comb, a brush, a toothbrush, soap, tooth powder, razor, and shaving soap. It will add to your comfort to bring one woolen blanket, preferably of dark or neutral color.[69]

Warns' monthly pay was $33, minus $6.50 per month for a $10,000 War Risk Insurance Policy.[70]

John Warns was twenty-three years old, but his induction papers do not include personal information such as his weight or height. The typical American soldiers "were small, in ill health, and poorly educated by the standards of the twenty-first century. The average soldier was twenty-two years of age, 5' 7" tall, and weighed 141 lbs. The median education for whites was 6.9 years, and 2.6 for blacks, with 31 percent testing illiterate."[71]

In 1916 Woodrow Wilson had been re-elected President largely on the basis of the slogan "He Kept Us Out Of War." It would have been just as accurate to proclaim "He Did Little to Prepare for The Possibility of War." In 1917 the armed forces of the United States ranked seventeenth in the world with just over one hundred thousand men. Since the United States declared war and *then* committed itself to building an army, the first draftees at Camp Funston in Kansas, where John Warns would spend most of his time in basic training, trained without uniforms and used wooden guns. Information compiled by the Keystone View Company and included on the backs of a set of World War I stereographs provides valuable insight into the training and war-time experience of Americans like John Warns. This information also gives us a first-hand look at wartime propaganda, an important element of the war effort on the war and home front. In the message which accompanies a stereograph entitled "Our Boys Responding To Uncle Sam's Call"" the rationale for a draft is explained as follows:

> April 28, 1917, marked a radical change in the military policy of the States. By the new army bill enacted at that time the old tradition of voluntary service had to give way to the more modern conscription. This measure gave the president power to raise an army of men to be selected by drafting those between twenty-one and thirty-one years of age. By the close of the war over four and one-half millions of men had been called for the army in this way. Voluntary service is not in keeping with the democratic principles of American government because it does not distribute the burden of military service equally.[72]

Wartime propaganda explained that "this was quite a problem for Uncle Sam when the United States entered the war. Our Government had never been faced with the problem of furnishing so many men with rifles. The great arms manufacturing companies had been so busy furnishing war supplies for the Allies that there was a rifle shortage."[73] By October of 1917 the United States was producing 1,200 Enfield rifles and 1,500 Springfield rifles a day. The Keystone View Company reported that the Enfield was the most effective and explained: "this is the gun that helped to whip the Hun and a very satisfactory weapon it proved to be when handled by the American doughboy."[74] Basic training at Camp Funston also provided bayonet training, which wartime propaganda referred to as "Learning How to Give the Huns a Taste of American Steel" and stereograph viewers were reminded that "if there is one thing the German fears more than anything else it is a bayonet charge."[75] The excellent physical condition of the soldiers is celebrated and is attributed to the "athletics and physical exercises, which form part of the army routine." After all "Uncle Sam realizes that the healthy solider will be a contented one and contented soldiers make few desertions, if any at all." The following was offered as evidence that the training program was a success: "Ex-President Roosevelt is so impressed with the physical, mental and moral development of the men in our national cantonments that he advocates the continuation of the camps after the war as permanent features of the life of all young men."[76] When it came to the training tables of the draftees, readers of the Keystone View Company material were informed that "Uncle Sam provides his soldiers with the best fare that can be bought in the country" and that American soldiers had appetites that "Rockefeller would envy."[77]

Wartime propaganda painted a rosy picture of departure for the conscription camps: "While love perhaps does bid the men to stay, they are really eager to enter camp. While there is a certain sadness in the breaking of the home ties, after three or four weeks of camp life most of the men would not go home to stay if they could." Women were admonished to refrain from making a "fuss" over the departure of their loved ones. And they were advised that if they could see how well the men were developing in the camps they would be "thankful that their sons and husbands were fine enough to be chosen to be a part of our splendid American army, the army upon which the safety of our republic depends." After all, this was the bottom line: "It is the attitude of the women at home that largely determines the morale of the boys at the front." Women were called upon to display their patriotism by embracing this maxim: "Love Bids Him Stay but Duty Calls to the Man in Khaki."[78]

From an undisclosed location on the way to Camp Funston, Kansas, John offered observations about the camp and indicated that he was tuned into President Wilson's ideological view of the war:

> Everybody feels good this morning for we just got notice that we had been transferred to Funston. No regrets here, this is really a rotten place at its best. When the dust blows you can't see 20 feet ahead of you. We have all kinds of fun here. Last night coming by the canteen a fellow come out with a cone in his right hand just as the officer came by. In his hurry to salute he lost his ice cream out of the cone, talk about laughing. Grub as a rule is good—if its poor at our kitchen we backslide over to the other kitchen. Its alright if you don't get caught you know. We have a lot of personal things to get even for aside of our fight for democracy. Looks as though I won't be back home for a while. We don't know when we leave but the 89th is ready for four hours' notice. We go to England and must be there in August for work, but we may be there June 1st.[79]

In May, 1918 Private Warns arrived in Camp Funston, Kansas, one of sixteen conscription camps around the United States.[80] Camp Funston had opened in the summer of 1917, and Major General Leonard Wood arrived that August. His mission was to turn new draftees into "Ninety Day Wonders." The first draftees arrived on 5 September, 1917 to begin formation of the Eighty-ninth Division of the United States Army. In his book entitled _The Doughboys_ Laurence Stallings made this observation:

> The 89th Division called itself the "Middle Wests" and was filled with men from the Canadian border to the Rio Grande, mountain men and trappers, cowboys from the plains, farm lads from the prairies and cornfields and

sundry characters from the ranches and deserts, again in
a roll call of states with beautiful names.[81]

They were also known as "Wood's Division." Warns made reference to General Wood when he noted that "this forenoon we march to Funston parade ground—our Battalion—and were reviewed by General Wood—he is back from France and papers are full of him. We walked by him columns of four looking "eyes right" and he had a smile for each of us. He sure is some general."[82] Warns' first impression of his new locale was not favorable: "The more I see of this damn country the more I think of S.D. as paradise. Nothing but rocks, hills and sand. One of our men picked up a grasshopper and upon post mortem examination found it had died of starvation."[83] Writing to his sister Anna, John described the travails of living in a tent: "Perhaps you think the wind blows out there. Well here they would call it a slight breeze. Last night the floor just raised off the ground and you can't see over 5 rods today. There's just about half an inch of dust on the floor and the beds and everything in the tent. You can't keep a thing on the wall, honest you folks can't realize how the sand blows here."[84] On May 3rd he reported, "I have my uniform now and say you wouldn't know me. . . . . I got two shots in the arm and feel like a whipped dog with a can on my tail. . . . . Damn those injections—that's another personal thing I've got against the Kaiser now." Warns described his uniform outfitting with sarcasm: "I got a good fit all around, my drawers are 36, I wear 42, my shirt 44, I wear 42, my pants are a little better but my blouse is a 40, 4 sizes too small as are my shoes. Oh it's great."[85] Warns' sarcastic commentary was corroborated in the *Brief History of the* 89th *Division*: "Although in the beginning there were no rifles, no uniforms, and insufficient buildings, the practical military training actually commenced on the first day."[86]

Camp Funston was unique among the sixteen training camps in that just outside the camp, an area known as the "Zone" was available to provide pleasant diversion from the rigors of drill. Author Joseph Mills Hanson explained:

This was a first-class pleasure resort with theaters, motion
picture houses, stores, and amusement arcade. The Zone

is said to have been the only enterprise of its kind created at any of the training camps. It was entirely developed and managed by a native South Dakotan, Mr. Maurice W. Jencks, formerly of Yankton, at the time one of the leading theatrical managers of the West.[87]

The variety of experiences available around Camp Funston probably provided quite a contrast to life on the farm near Wentworth. Warns also referred to activities designed to entertain and build morale: "We have boxing matches baseball and singing." Movies were shown at the YMCA and he enjoyed the food: "We had beef steak, spuds, green peas, bread, ice cream and water."[88] And John's sense of humor had not been dampened by basic training:

> Yesterday we got two magnesium sulphate pills each and last night the entire company made a flank attack on the latrine which proved successful. Gas played a big part in the attack and several got overcome. Others were forced to wash their underwear this morning vainly attempting to get the trench dirt and beans out of them. The guards reported gas odors as far as a mile away from the object of attack, the enemy consisted of six stools.[89]

Private John Warns was now one of approximately one-hundred and seventy men who comprised the Machine Gun Company of the 355th Infantry within the larger Eighty-ninth Division (10,000 to 15,000 men), and he noted, "Boys coming in and going all the time. Guess we will learn as fast as possible and we sure are willing." The 355th Infantry left Camp Funston for New York with less than thirty days of training, but it was enough time for Private Warns, with the bravado of a new recruit, to observe, "The Machine Gun Company is, according to Lieutenant McBride, the snappiest damn company in the whole damn army. We're proud of it."[90] On 28 May, 1918 Private Warns, who had previously never ventured far from the family farm at Wentworth, described his arrival in New York City, and his fascination with the Statue of Liberty:

> When we got into N.Y. we were marched to the Ferry
> Station and crossed the Hudson Bay. It's about five miles
> across. We went under the Brooklyn Bridge-the largest
> bridge in the U.S. I guess. My first taste of salt water
> agreed with me about as much as castor oil does. But oh
> the thrill of seeing the Statue of Liberty. I can't describe
> how I felt, but looking up to this great imposing statue
> just makes one feel safe—that's about as near as I can
> come to it.[91]

The entire Eighty-ninth Division was gathering at Camp Mills, on Long Island New York as 278, 644 United States troops were scheduled to leave for Europe in June.[92] Private Warns had this to say about the impending trip "Over There":

> Somehow going over don't worry me in the least as far as
> myself is concerned. I feel just as though I were leaving
> for a little trip tomorrow. And I haven't worried about
> myself since I left home. I feel safe and at home wher-
> ever I rest my-sometimes darn-dreary-head—but I can't
> help thinking sometimes that the 30 days gone bye are
> altogether too short for training even though we have
> learned—actually learned—more than former recruits
> learned in three months, and we will have a good deal of
> training "over there."[93]

On the home front, pressure to support the war effort intensified as American troops sailed for Europe. Three incidents in the Wentworth area during the spring of 1918 indicate the extent to which support for the war effort had been twisted into a mindless frenzy. The first involved Geo. Ohlinger of rural Madison, South Dakota who had refused to contribute to the Red Cross, had not signed up for a Liberty Loan, or supported any other patriotic causes. The *Wentworth Enterprise* reported in a front-page story that a number of persons had gathered at Ohlinger's farm "and applied an irregular decoration of yellow paint to his build-ings." The newspaper related that many automobile loads of people had made the fourteen-mile trip to view this violation of Ohlinger's property. The *Enterprise* concluded this story with a morality lesson for all to heed: "Ohlinger came to Madison today and signed up for Liberty Bonds to an amount satisfactory to the committee, and the incident may therefore be considered closed."[94]

The second incident took place in May when yellow paint was applied to the south front and the west windows of the German Lutheran Parochial School in Wentworth, South Dakota. The *Wentworth Enterprise* sought to shift the blame for this incident to outsiders when it claimed, "Many are of the opinion that it was done by out-of-town parties." But even the staunchly patriotic newspaper suggested that things had gone too far, noting that, "It is the general opinion among our citizens that a wrong has been done. Members of the congregation have lately proved themselves quite loyal in all war activities, having donated liberally to the Red Cross, and as a whole were not deserving of such treatment." However, the newspaper did explain that the German language was still being taught in the school, a practice that "is to be discontinued at the close of this term, we are informed."[95] When Private John Warns was made aware that the Parochial School he had attended had been desecrated in the name of patriotism, he voiced his disgust to his sister Anna: "So they painted the schoolhouse yellow—if I were there somebody would get tarred and feathered. Have you any suspicions? The boys here are all against mob rule and there's talk of sending soldiers wherever they have trouble."[96]

The third incident took place in June of 1918. The *Wentworth Enterprise* reported that "a rather disgusting affair occurred in our city late last Saturday night when a mob caught and horse-whipped Carl Meyer, for the past several years a mail carrier on Route Three out of this place." The cause of this incident appeared to be "the attitude shown by Mr. Meyer towards our several war activities, and his failure to report at the meeting on War Savings Day." The chairman of the War Savings Day event had informed Meyer that if he was not going to purchase stamps, he would have to indicate how many he had already purchased. Meyer's recorded response was "that he did not think it was necessary for him to tell the whole United States how many stamps he had." The Saturday night mob was not aware that Meyer had signed a pledge card earlier that evening. The newspaper expressed regret that the incident had taken place, but suggested "it must remain as an example to those who might wrongly believe that they can take an indifferent and sometimes opposing stand toward the activities of our government in the prosecution of the war in which we are engaged."[97] When coupled with the controversy surrounding the Nonpartisan League, these three events make it clear that there was no room for dissent in Wentworth, South Dakota. Intolerance had truly become an American "virtue", a "virtue" now in vogue in even the most rural and isolated areas of the United States.

As these three events troubled the community of Wentworth, the reality of his departure for Europe loomed heavily on John's mind as he wrote to Anna:

> Dear Anna: Got your letter this evening and no letter I re-
> ceived so far really cheered me up so much. Make mother
> feel the same way about it as you do. I am Uncle Sam's
> boy and I owe my country my services. The fitter I am as I
> enter the better are my chances for coming out fit. There's
> absolutely no need for worry. I can't write much—how-
> ever we are all packed awaiting orders, however we may
> be here till morning at that. You asked why I needed the
> money—I wanted to take it over in draft for emergencies
> over there tobacco cost 35 cents a can, matches 25 cents—
> see? However it hasn't reached me yet so I'll have to go
> without—and durn it I'm all out of Velvet at that. Glad
> the hail didn't hurt the crops. Rained here like the dickens
> at the same time awful hot today. Cool now. Well so long
> Anna and don't let that Saxon get hurt because both hands
> aren't on the wheel. I owe George a letter too.[98]

On 4 June 1918 Private John Warns sailed with the Eighty-ninth Division from New York onboard the White Star Line Ship *Baltic*.[99] While in route for England Private Warns' spirits were high as he wrote, "Am sure enjoying myself and feeling prouder every day of the Machine Gun Co. I tell you folks when we get started the Kaiser is going to move by force. We sure have some hard-boiled guys in this Co. I'm afraid I'll be somewhat hard boiled myself before I get back. We have a bunch of sergeants that every man in the company would stick to until the last."[100] Warns reminded his family that he was "hale and hearty" and attempted to calm his family's apprehensions: "Do hope the U-boats don't worry you—every precaution is taken and there's no danger hardly at all—or don't worry about it Mother." All of them would have to take refuge in their faith: "God will take care of us here as well as in camp or at home and everyone else is trying to take care of us also."[101] The *Baltic* arrived in England on 16 June, 1918.[102]

Warns' first letter from Europe is characterized by a shift in tone and mood, and the extent to which letters from home will sustain him in the coming months becomes clear. Writing directly to his mother, Dora, he remarks that he has reread her letter "fifty times or more though I know it by heart." He points out that he has "had time to think of many things I've never thought of before, and I miss you so often, but then I see old gray headed mothers here who have lost everything. I feel as though I own the world." He continues by describing a dream he had on the fourth day out at sea: "I dreamt of you. You were telling me something that cheered me up—but I can't think of what it was. I only know I woke up all cheered up, only to find it was a dream. I can feel you thinking and praying for me now and it helps mother dear . . . . . Write me often mamma <u>and write</u> <u>yourself</u> and tell Dad to write also."[103]

From England John Warns wrote to Anna and described the bucolic countryside, noted that some of the people lived in the same buildings with their livestock, pointed out that the people welcomed the arrival of Americans, and expressed his desire to return to England after the war:

> Just how I like this country would be hard to tell. Flowers are blooming everywhere, never seen so many flowers in one place. The houses are all of brick and nearly all alike and covered with vines. The climate is cool here but not cold. It was cold tho where we were at before. The grain is headed out and potatoes and beans look as tho they are ready to eat. One thing is especially noticeable namely the fine cattle horses and sheep. I noticed very few hogs and those I seen were poor grade. But oh such herds of cattle-one just like the other and sheep that roamed make ours look like saints. Some of the tenants live in the same

buildings with the stock. Flowers are on one side of the house, wheel barrow on the other. The people seem to welcome us-especially the women folks cheered continually as we went through. The greatest encouragement however were the old people smiling and nodding at us. They seemed to say "we're depending on you" and you can bet your sweet life they are sitting safe, for we are going to finish up right before we get through. And oh when we get back!! But I'm not all sure but what-if possible-I'll take my time going back and see England. The old Roman ruins and chapels are something I must see while I'm here.[104]

Just a few days later John had visited the ruins of an abbey and he described their evocative impact: "I wish you could have been with me and that we could spend an entire day in there. It's a monstrous building, part of it was built in 907 by the Romans, and the English added to it as the years went by." His encounter with this medieval structure moved him to ponder: "It is such a large, quiet place to worship in and I wondered how many had been there in ages gone by with their troubles." He admitted that he was homesick for news and asked, "How are the crops and the pigs? Wish to God I had some fried eggs of those I ate when I didn't need them. Although we are getting enough to eat, there are so many things we can't get—eggs and sweets and pastries, etc." He closed this letter by saying "I'll go over to the Y hall and listen to the program. Have a ball game every evening, but I was too tired to go tonight. Am writing this in the Y, and its here we get our newspapers, books and everything we need." John once again reassured his family that he was "hale and hearty." [105]

Private Warns' first-hand descriptions of basic training at Camp Funston provide a realistic counterpoint to the version espoused by sources such as the Keystone Company Stereograph propaganda. And while the relentless drive to demand support for the war effort continued to erupt into controversy in Wentworth, John Warns had faithfully responded to the war-time draft, providing tangible proof of his patriotism. After thirty days of state-side training, and a trans-Atlantic voyage to England, Warns and the Eighty-ninth Division were poised to enter the most destructive war zone the world had ever experienced—the Western Front of World War One.

CHAPTER FOUR

Western Front

"Agnes says she was so angry she'd shot at the screen had she had a revolver."
-Anna Warns

lthough American troops had first arrived in Europe in 1917, and
previously provided distinguished service at places like Belleau
Wood in June of 1918, it would be the striking power of a massive
American Expeditionary Force in the Saint Mihiel and Meuse-Argonne
offensives that would inject American military might into the allied side
of the Western Front, enabling a swift conclusion to the war in November,
1918. Private John Warns, and his 355th Infantry of the Eighty-ninth
Division played key roles in each of these offensives. John's letters provide
realistic eye-witness accounts of these war front battles, while from the
home front, letters from his family and Lutheran pastor sustained John
through the duration of the hostilities.

While millions of Europeans cheered the arrival of troops from the
United States, tensions quickly developed between the American General
John J. Pershing and the British and French. The Allied powers had been
fighting off a massive German offensive since March of 1918, and German
troops were just forty miles from Paris. Despite Allied pleas that American
troops be immediately mixed among British and French troops in the
front line, Pershing had another idea. He was understandably reluctant

to turn control of American troops over to an alliance that had been engaging in nearly four years of destructive and indecisive trench warfare. Pershing's military strategy was also linked to President Wilson's political and diplomatic vision—a strong and decisive display of American military might would ensure an important role for the United States in the postwar peace negotiations.[106] In May of 1918, Pershing reminded the Allies that the United States had declared war independently—as an Associated Power, known as the American Expeditionary Forces. Pershing explained that it would take time to train a powerful army, and he insisted "that the morale of the soldiers depends upon fighting under our own flag."[107] Lloyd George of England disagreed and expressed his fear that if American troops were not immediately sent to the front, the war would end with a German victory. For the most part Pershing stood his ground, while offering this compromise: in May of 1918, 130,000 American troops entered the front line. Another 150,000 did the same in June. However, two-thirds of the American troops would not go to the front until they could do so as an American army, a goal that would take until 30 August to achieve. Pershing strategized that 1918 would feature a build-up of American troops in Europe, and in 1919 these troops would be used to bring a decisive end to the war.[108]

For its part in this amassing of American military might on the Western Front, the Eighty-ninth Division took trains across England to Southampton, and between June 20th and 29th, they were transported across the English Channel to Le Havre, France. After a two-day rest, trains took the Eighty-ninth through the outskirts of Paris on a two-day ride to an area ten miles northeast of Chaumont. The 355 Infantry of the Eighty-ninth Division was headquartered at the villages of Grand, Brechainville and Aillianville. Six weeks of training took place at these locations.[109] Sometime between John's letter of 21 June 1918 and a letter written 9 July 1918, Warns was hospitalized for an undisclosed illness (perhaps mumps), and he wrote to Anna (nicknamed Tommy) from "Somewhere in France", describing his medical treatment and requesting updates on events from the home front:

> Well Tommy I presume there's oceans of letters waiting
> for me somewhere but they haven't reached me so I'll send

one instead even tho there's not much to tell: My musings are mostly a sore throat today as the swelling has gone down completely and this noon I go on regular diet which means Ill soon be out. Were it not for loosing so much time and training I would feel sorry, for it sure is great to sleep on a mattress and between sheets and have a feather pillow—The first pillow I slept on since I left home. And this resting is medicine in itself.

I was thinking of what there's going on back home about this time. Have you had a circus and How's the Chautauqua? Have you one in Wentworth? I presume now that you drive the car you can go to any of 'em or do you wait for the Saxon? ha-ha. By the way how are the Sioux City Tires holding out and have you any more trouble with the ignition?

How's politics down there? I presume dad is getting downright interested. Is P.A.J. running for auditor? And have Mattie or Sudan been around lately?[110]

On the home front, propaganda had a major role in galvanizing popular support for U. S. entry into the war, and for maintaining morale and unity during the war years. Beginning in 1917 the *Wentworth Enterprise* featured an anti-German cartoon on the front page of its weekly publication and the names of all the men who had contributed to the Liberty Loan drive were also published on the front page.[111] On the national level the Committee of Public Information "promoted movies like *The Prussian Cur,* and *The Kaiser, the Beast of Berlin.*"[112] Private Warns' sister Anna, wrote a letter to John that he received while he was receiving medical treatment. Anna and some of her friends had just been to nearby Madison, South Dakota to see the movie entitled *Over the Top.*[113] Anna referred to the Germans as "Huns" and the riveting impact the movie had on Anna's emotions clearly illustrates the extent to which the propaganda efforts of the Committee of Public Information had reached rural South Dakota:

I mentioned in my letter yesterday that R. A. was going to take me to see "Over the Top" at Madison. Well we went, Laura, Agnes myself, and R. A. and such a show.

I wouldn't take a million for the two hours spent there. I thought the Birth of a Nation was good but this was great. There hasn't any thing affected me as that play did for ages. Hope you'll have the honor of going "Over the Top" as "Garry" did. Saw a machine gun in motion. Some little cracker jack ain't it. I'm wishing all the time now that I were a boy. Bet your book I'd be with the colors. By July I'm going to try and get a chance to get in this last Red Cross nurse call but don't ask questions in your letters, as this is a secret between you and me. You know what I mean don't you? R. A. is an alternate and will probably go anyway Friday. He wants to awfully bad. Gee I can't keep my thoughts from the play I wish I could give you a whole account of it. Those darn German officers. Would like to have had the chance to kill some of them. Agnes says she was so angry that she'd have shot at the screen had she had a revolver. A play like that one is worth seeing. Want the folks to go tonight but don't know whether they will or not.

I remain,

Lovingly

Sister Tommy

P.S. When you get ready to shoot grapefruit [shot] at the Huns with the M. G. give them an extra dose for me.[114]

"Anna Warns"

On the back of this photo, Anna wrote, "This will give you an idea of how stuck up I am since I am working for Uncle Sam. Ha ha. Guess I have my head up to high any way. Ha ha. Say, what are you doing now? Suppose you made a list of every French girl you saw. Ha ha. Your pictures haven't come yet, be sure to send us the address of the place. Dad is hauling in alfalfa hay today, its dandy. Crops look good. We have the best corn for miles around."

Anna, who was eighteen years old in 1918, helped with John's mail route while he was at war, purchased her own horse and buggy and substituted for other mail carriers.[115] She once wrote to him saying: "Say pardon me for getting angry at you when you returned from the mail route, lazy. I'm so darn tired tonight I can hardly see straight ha ha, . . . We get a raise this month, don't know how much but they say some near $4.00."[116] From the Base Hospital "Somewhere in France" John expressed his frustration with his hospitalization to his sister "Tommy": "I don't feel like doing anything, this inaction is getting on my nerves for a fact." While hundreds of thousands of hungry boys were fighting day and night within a few miles, it bothered John that he had a "real bed and three-square meals a day doing nothing. I feel rotten about it and the nurse tells me we are here for two weeks more." John's thoughts then turned to politics and the controversy surrounding the NPL: "Tell dad to find out about the arrangements for voting for I want to vote on the state and county ticket", "I presume politics are waging hot again. Is that pro-German aristocrat still mayor in Madison? Wish I had him here. Bless me if I wouldn't force him over the top with my colts prodding him in the ribs."[117] The very next day John wrote to Anna to assure her that she and the Warns family should not worry about him, and he made it clear that he was not comfortable with the recognition he was receiving from his home congregation, Saint Peter's Lutheran Church in Wentworth:

> Good bye and folks—don't worry—I'm just as dam safe here as I am at home, and I feel I will be back. Wont that be some day for us tho—It won't be this year but it won't take long. And it's harder in a material way on you there then it is on me. Think of the advantage I have—White bread, milk, sugar, and meals. Constant doctors care, healthy exercise and just enough hard work to make me appreciate sleep each night. About the only thing I miss is news and letters. And tobacco. Lutheran pastors and the Red Cross, Y.M.C.A. all take care of us, so why worry?
>
> I'm out of the medicine now but won't need any more. However I still have the nose bleed quite often. Who in the saints name is the service flag for? Aint I the only one out of the church. If they want to do something have 'em subscribe to the Red Cross again. This having a service flag for one person is dam foolishness.[118]

On 6 August, 1918 Warns wrote to his Mother Dora "to let you know that I am hale and hearty and back with my company." He was still "bothered by colic and nosebleed but am getting over it."[119] One day later an incident occurred that would change John's "hale and hearty" status and impact him for the rest of his life. Private Warns was one of five hundred

and fifty-six men of the Eighty-ninth Division who were exposed to poisonous gas on the night of 7-8 August. Forty-two officers and men were
killed.[120] In letters written later in August and September, Warns briefly
mentions a hospital stay, but it is difficult to determine if he is referring to
his July visit to a hospital, or a post-poisonous gas exposure hospital stay
in August. It is certain that his exposure to mustard gas caused Private
Warns to be categorized as "disabled" after his post-war discharge from
the army, and that he suffered life-long health problems related to this
war-time experience.

Later in 1918, Warns wrote to "Tommy" [Anna] from Grosslittgen,
Germany detailing how he had rejoined the 355th after his time in the
hospital. He explained that the pictures of himself that he was sending had
been taken in July. On his way back to the Western Front he had spent
time in Saint Aignan, "south of Paris—a big town—wonderful scenery."
After seeing several other towns he reported, "I got back to my company
just three days before we went in the trenches below Seicheprey."[121] On 2
September, 1918 John wrote to "Dear Mother and all", and his reference to
"work's all done up" probably indicates that he was no longer hospitalized.
He expressed his thanks to his Uncle Paul for "three packs of cigarettes"
he received in the mail and reported that he had recently "attended the
Salvation Army service and prayers were exceptionally good." By now
John was becoming more nostalgic as his thoughts turned to what he was
missing back home: "Somehow I feel like going duck hunting. How are
the sloughs and are there many ducks? I presume thrashing is well started,
am anxious to know how the grain runs. Seems really odd to see a summer
go by without getting in the grain fields."[122] On the larger strategic scale,
the 355 Infantry was about to become involved in one of the two major
Allied offensives of 1918.

While military strategists were planning the St. Mihiel offensive,
the Eighty-ninth Division held a ten-mile section of the south side of the
Saint Mihiel salient, located approximately twenty-two miles southeast of
Verdun.[123] The salient was a "strongly fortified" two hundred square mile
"triangular indentation into the Western Front" that the Germans had held
for four years.[124] It was essential to any future offensives that this salient be
reduced in order to prevent German counter-attacks. Holding this position
proved costly to the Eighty-ninth. By 21 August forty-two officers and men

had died as a result of gas poisoning. During this thirty-two-day stretch, the division "lost more men wounded than during the offensive itself, and almost as many total causalities, the figures being eighty-six officers and men killed or died of wounds and seven-hundred and twenty-eight wounded."[125] The Saint Mihiel offensive would be the first independent movement conducted by the American First Army, which had been officially formed on 30 August, 1918. Pershing was determined to mount a successful first offensive, and the forces he assembled outnumbered the Germans in the salient four to one. Private Warns wrote "I presume you have heard of the big drive going on and the great success we are having. Telegraph messages coming in yesterday, according to the Lieutenant, tell of just uncomprehendable numbers of prisoners. Haven't seen the evening paper yet. Last night the big guns could plainly be heard."[126] Private Warns described this situation from near the French village of Aneauville:

Of course there's no dodging around it—-you know it anyhow- sometimes it isn't so pleasant, especially when one sits up for hours at a time with a gas mask on in a night so dark ink would show up white. One realizes a little of the danger and when the guns vibrate the ground one just does get a wee bit nervous and excited—Mother dear—one sure thinks of a lot of things in a blessed little time during occasions of this kind, and were it not for knowing that the Lord knows where you are and is taking care of you, one would feel like a fly on tanglefoot lost. I wrote of losing all the pictures and your letters, they slipped out of my pocket, I saw them drop but we couldn't stop, I had my name in them—perhaps someone will pick them up and return them. I sure felt blue about it, now I haven't a picture or a letter or anything.[127]

The following day, Sunday 11 August, 1918, John wrote to Anna "celebrating again today for your letters of June 24th and July 5th got here this morning and it was the first mail I got for ages." He offered these observations about life on the Western Front:

This morning I went with a bunch of others to the nearby village to get a bath and change underwear - and while there went up to the Salvation Army hut to get paper, etc. got some candy, dried currents and a bottle of beer. When I got back I soaked my dirty clothes—in an empty can and after dinner done the family washing consisting of a suit of underwear, 2 pairs of socks, 3 towels, 4 handkerchiefs and a shirt—in an old shell hole filled with water. Oh Mother if you could have seen me—sleeves rolled up, shirt open, sweat streaming down my face and soapsuds splattered around a dozen feet each way—but my clothes look real fine—am drying em in the sun to bleach.

The woods are quiet today with the exception of a few artillery shots once in a while. One can find all kinds of junk for souvenirs here but as one can't carry it one leaves it lay. One of the boys found a brass barreled revolver. Helmets and swords have been found by several. The Germans occupied these woods once upon a time they say. Have run across lots of shell holes bigger than our cellar, but they are all old. Outside of gas alarms and aircraft battles there's nothing doing here. Our Stars and Stripes came today and I note that we are supposed to be either in heaven—hell—or Hoboken by Christmas—who knows?

I got mothers bill and dads draft for $25—the latter at the hospital.

I'm afraid I can't get you a French sister in law—for I haven't seen madamasell for over six weeks and am God knows how far away from her—She promised to write—if she does I'll have to get one of the French soldiers here to read it,—for I've quit learning—gave it up as being an occupation not necessary for the successful conclusion of the war—ha-ha![128]

Warns' next letter reveals details about the intensity of front line combat, his observation of the air war, his opportunity to see General Pershing, his responsibility for loading the machine guns with ammunition, and his hospitalization. Warns uses "Fritz" as a slang term to refer to the Germans, and like his sister Anna in her June 1918 letter, Warns also refers to the Germans as "Huns":

> Last night it was quiet the moonlight was so bright one could have read papers. I was laying a dreaming for a long while when all at once hell popped loose- but just for a few moments. Fritz was considerate for he done it early. Usually he routs us out when we are nicely asleep. We have had several gas alarms but no gas. Talk about sport-wearing the mask isn't in it. One night at the gun Fritz sent over some shrapnel and one exploded so close stray pieces fell within 5 yards of us. I recon I know how to hug anyhow I never hugged anything closer in my life as I did the ground and I'll vow it would have taken a ton of dynamite to move me for the following few minutes. – I wasn't scared – nosiree not a bit- just felt chilly all over For real excitement however there's nothing I've seen that beats a airplane battle. I've seen a number of them and I can't describe the thrilling sensation of watching them dive, flop and spin around sometimes so high one can hardly see them, so far have seen two Hun machines brought down the way they tumble down and hit the ground is a sight one never forgets. Must mention another unusual incident- the place we are at now was evacuated by the company Pierre Weisse is in. He told me all about this county and I found it just as he described it. Reckon he is back with his outfit for he left the hospital two day before I did. If he is, he is up where the big fight is. Did I tell about seeing General Pershing the day I left the casual camp? He sure is some man. No wonder everyone likes him- one couldn't help respecting and liking him.

He passed about six feet from me and was smiling all the time.

Tell Anna her letter cheered me up wonderfully- and I'll sure send over a few shots for her if I ever get on the gun. My work is filling the belts- it's just as important but more tiresome and not half interesting enough. We all carry a colt 7 shot automatic on our belt for protection in fact when I'm all rigged up I look like a Christmas tree. I carry a Sola scabbard canteen and cup and cover, first aid packet, two cartridge pouches, automatic and holster gloves all on my belt without the pack and helmet. I've discarded all my personal stuff except the toilet pouch. Gave my extra blanket to the Red Cross and threw my other stuff in the woods. Signed up for pay some days ago and will send most of it home for dad to do with as he sees fit.- Have still some of the draft dad sent me. Well I guess I'll have to ring up. Will be where its more interesting before you get this letter but it's a quiet sector so don't worry and write often, especially do I miss mother's letters she writes so little and dad hasn't written since I left the hospital. As ever John.[129]

By late August Private Warns had been at the front for several weeks and in an eight-page letter he refers to many of the aspects of life in the trenches. At 12:30 AM, 22 August Warns wrote "Fritz sends over greetings regular and especially at meal time. Seems funny to hear em explode—sometimes really to close for comfort." Rats were frequent, unwanted guests in the trenches, and Warns observed that, "Harry sure can get all the rat hides he wants here—they are not muskrats, but they are damn near as big and as thick as flies. I wouldn't walk around in the dugout without shoes on for love or money." In a recent letter sister Anna had requested more direct details about the war, but Warns responded, "Can't be done Tommy, for the really interesting things I've seen are just the things the damn Huns want to know about and I'm not going to give em a chance to learn anything. I'll tell you all about it when I get back."

Warns had found some time to tour the area and remarked, "Yes I've seen quite a few palaces. Read up on Joan of Arc—I've seen the place she was born and Queen Louise—seen her palace and a palace where an old king, forgot what his John Henry was, got his head cut off. They buried his head in the church in the same place." He closed his letter by writing "I'll just crawl in for a good night's sleep—I share my bed with rats and I hear them already in the bed."[130]

Private Warns managed to deal with his distressing circumstances through support from home and a reliance on his Christian faith. In letters dated 29 August and 9 September, 1918, Warns wrote: "Pray often for me mother—I know your prayers have helped me all along and I need them in the future, but don't quit at praying, quit worrying also."[131] The twin themes of religious piety and intense patriotism were common in letters to Warns written by Uncle Jake, a Wentworth resident who owned land and worked as a demolition contractor. On 11 September, 1918 Uncle Jake noted that, "From all the newspaper reports we see the boys are making good and pushing the Germans back to beat the band. Don't it make you feel good to be one of them that accomplished this, and is it not a glorious feeling to know that you have been a part in this great army that is making the world sit up and take notice. And isn't it a source of satisfaction to know that you have done your duty? I should say yes." Uncle Jake reminded Private Warns of his religious upbringing in the Lutheran faith: "You don't get a chance now at all to go to a church of our faith. But be sure and read your bible regularly, you will find something interesting every time, and what's more you will find comfort and peace. Here's where you have an advantage over many others, who know nothing about God and his love for poor sinners, know not how to live right and die happy in the faith of Christ."[132]

"Private John Warns with his Bible"

It had been determined that the St. Mihiel Offensive would begin on 12 September, 1918. In order to maintain as much secrecy as possible, the American troops moved to the southern side of the salient by night and were forced to take cover and sleep during the day.[133] The night of September 11th was pitch black with a steady rain.[134] At 1:00 AM on 12 September, a four-hour artillery bombardment of the German positions began. In a twentieth anniversary reflection on the offensive, Warns' 355th Infantry's role was vividly recounted: "We are in the trenches fronting the St. Mihiel salient. It is cold, rainy and dismal. The trenches are filled with water and mud and the roads are congested with moving troops, guns and supply trains. All seems confusion and disorder. The St. Mihiel push is about to shove off! But there is no thrill of coming conflict. For we are tired."[135] At 5:00 AM the Eighty-ninth Division went "over the top" near Remieres Wood and the village of Seicheprey.[136] They encountered a German army that was, in some instances in retreat, but in others offering stiff resistance. By 6:00 PM on September 12 the 355th Infantry was digging in and on the verge of exhaustion, since many had marched all of the previous night and some the night before that. Upon entering the salient the Eight-ninth Division became eyewitnesses to the carnage of war as they encountered hundreds of fires from military stores and supplies, timid civilians emerging from their hiding places after four years of German occupation, huge kettles of warm food left by retreating Germans and the evidence of destruction caused by the pre-offensive artillery bombardment:

> The road from Bouillonville to Thiaucourt presented a gruesome sight. A wagon train moving out supplies had evidently been caught there in our fire. The bodies of many German soldiers lay in the road itself, and the hillside above, over which they had attempted to flee, was thickly strewn with corpses. In the road were many loaded wagons, the horses lying dead in the harness, twisted into grotesque shapes by the fearful explosions.[137]

Twenty years later, an anniversary account stated, "We toil up from the dark valley and before us lies a scene to stir the emotions. Far to the southwest, in the angle of the old St. Mihiel salient—now no longer a salient—blazes hundreds of fires. They are from military stores and supplies, barracks and villages which the defeated enemy seeks to prevent falling into our hands. We are touched by the greetings of the civilians who have clung to their homes. They come, half stunned and starved, from their hiding places and their feelings are almost too deep for expression. They reach out and touch us timidly."[138]

During the offensive, the Eighty-ninth Division captured 2,207 regular German troops and took eighty officers prisoner, while suffering losses of 214 men killed.[139] On 13 September, 1918 General Pershing celebrated his 58th birthday by escorting French General Henri-Philippe Petain to the liberated village of St. Mihiel. The offensive had proven that the Americans could mount an independent attack and appeared to vindicate Pershing's earlier insistence that the majority of Americans would fight independently from the Allies. Strategically, the Germans had been deprived of a base "from which they could have harassed the rear of the American force during the upcoming Meuse-Argonne Offensive."[140] In a telegram General Pershing commended the Eighty-ninth Division for its "courageous dash and vigor" which "thrilled our countrymen and invoked the enthusiasm of our Allies." Pershing took "soldierly pride" in the Eighty-ninth Division's liberation of "two-hundred and forty square miles of French territory":

> On September 12th, 1918, you delivered the first concerted offensive operation of the American Expeditionary Forces upon difficult terrain against this redoubtable position, immovably held for four years which crumbled before our ably executed advance. Within 24 hours of the commencement of the attack, the salient had ceased to exist... you have demonstrated the fitness for battle of a unified American Army.[141]

Thirteen days later Warns reported almost giddily on going "over the top", explained how it was he had forgotten that he was a prohibition supporter, and made reference to the NPL/Norbeck contested gubernatorial election of 1918:

> Dearest folks: - Well we've been "over the top" and I'm writing this letter on a table on which probably a German "officer" ate his bread and drank this Rhine wine. When they left they left quite a little wine behind and I'm telling the world I forgot all about being a prohibition booster until I was reminded of it by the wine giving out. Also enjoyed a few "officer" cigars- they were real good in comparison to the cabbage they have for the "soldat" I wish I could describe the drive- the barrage, etc., but I reckon it would be hard to tell if I could. Sorry to say the only Germans I saw running were hardly in sight through a field glass- but folks- I sure don't blame em for running. Talk about noise- well words can't describe it and as I wrote before- Got away without a scratch and am in the pink of condition in spite of wet weather and a few sleepless nights. I got a can of Tuxedo from the Red Cross just as it was beginning to get on my nerves so I loaded my pipe and steamed it off. Say dad you'll never be able to tell me there's nothing but a habit to smoking. Next to a fervent prayer I reckon there's nothing that will put one

more at ease. Uncle Paul's advice to go low on the smoking habit won't have a chance for trial here. Ha ha… I see by the clippings that politics are playing a big part in our state- I get an Argus Leader once in a while and them and the clippings I can see that it will be some fight. However I hear little of Gov Norbeck - don't he ever say anything?[142]

When Warns sent items home that he had collected during the Saint Mihiel offensive he explained to "Tommy" [Anna] "the silk scarf is part of an officer's pack. The officers left in a hurry. His pocket knife was on the table—with a cork in the corkscrew." Warns also provided a geographical reference that indicated the location of the 355th Infantry; "This was at Beney [Beney-en Woevre] on the St. Mihiel drive. I have the knife also. Be sure to save the scarf for me."[143]

On the very day that this letter was dated (26 September, 1918), the Meuse-Argonne Offensive had been launched approximately thirty-five miles to the northwest of the Eighty-ninth division's location. This was the second offensive to feature major involvement by the American Expeditionary Forces, and the last major offensive of World War One. For the first twelve days of this offensive, the Eighty-ninth Division remained in the former St. Mihiel salient and held the line along a ten-mile front near the village of Rembrecourt, with the 355th Infantry located near the village of Xammes. Casualties continued at a steady pace as 165 members of the division were killed in action.[144] By 3 October 1918 Private Warns observed "The daily papers sure look good now. A rumor just told us that Bulgaria came to her senses and quit. Just so the Kaiser don't quit before we've pounded the devil out of him."[145] On 7 and 8 October, 1918 the Eighty-ninth was part of a force of 400,000 men that began moving from St. Mihiel to join the Meuse-Argonne Offensive and once again they traveled at night and slept by day.[146] Located on the southern edge of the war's final offensive, the Meuse-Argonne region featured formidable defensive terrain that was "vital to Germany because it protected the railroad that supplied at least the southern half of their front line troops."[147] By 13 October the Eighty-ninth had marched to Mountfaucon and spent the night. Within a few days the Eighty-ninth was in combat near the villages of Cunel and Romagne. On 20 October, Warns and his 355th infantry and the 356[148] infantry were ordered to move forward to "clean up thoroughly the woods" in the Bois de Bantheville region, which was "still held in force" by the Germans, with the 355th infantry meeting stubborn resistance.[148] From Oldham, South Dakota, school-teacher Ida Rottluf wrote to Warns to tell him that she had heard an optimistic report from the Western Front via her cousin Julius: "The way he writes he doesn't think the war will last much longer. Well, I hope he's a good guesser, if it ends the right way. The papers sure look encouraging. Haven't the Belgians been doing splendid work the last week?" Ida asked Warns, "Are you still living in your happy home, the dug-out? Or are you moving Rhineward with the rest of the Yanks?" She also informed Warns that the influenza epidemic had reached Oldham: "The schools were closed on account of the influenza, so I am having a little vacation, I don't know how much longer it will last, maybe a week or two."[149]

On 23 October, 1918 Warns wrote to his sister Dorothy (Dimples) "we all must suffer and sacrifice for the sake of liberty and our country and I feel confident that it won't take much more to knock Kaiserism to the devil. All we can do is pray and fight."[150] On 17 October 1918, Warns wrote that he still figured he would be home for Christmas dinner "for everything seems to indicate that the Huns are whipped and peace seems only a matter of weeks." However, he explained that just in case he did not make it home, he was sending a detailed list of what he hoped would be sent to him in his Christmas box.[151]

Warns also expressed interest in South Dakota's 5 November, 1918 gubernatorial election in which he favored the NPL's Bates rather than the incumbent, Peter Norbeck:

> I've got the ballot but am still carrying it with me. Am afraid I won't be able to vote—have seen nothing permitting it. Sure would like to do my bit and help Bates in. He is the right man for Governor and every patriotic man will vote for him. Well politics shouldn't worry me, what's worrying me is the ability to get a first class suite on the boat that points west. Last night I was dreaming of having a brand new fur cap with a collar on it. It was the warmest thing I ever had on. I woke up to find three mice nestled

up against my neck and cheek. It was raining outside so I guess a pup tent looked as good to them as it does to me. I never seen a place where there were more field mice than are here. They are in your clothing as soon as you lay it on the ground, and they are about three times as big as the mice back home. They are pretty looking and quite tame. One can catch them by just reaching for them.[152]

Although the controversy over the NPL and the harsh treatment of "slackers" had divided the community of Wentworth, South Dakota, Warns did find support from his home congregation at Saint Peter's Lutheran Church. In October 1918 Private Warns received a lengthy letter from his pastor, Ferinand Oberheu, written in response to a letter he had received from John. Pastor Oberheu assured John that "we here at home think and speak of our boys out in the trenches and in the camp often and remember them in our prayer." He told Warns that his home congregation had dedicated a "service flag" with 13 stars for each man from the church who was serving in the military, and that the flag was hung "not in a hidden corner, where nobody may see it, no we hung it in a place, where the eyes of all who come to this church must see it." Pastor Oberheu proceeded to offer his theological perspective on war:

When the country calls the Christian to the colors, he does respond, not for the sake of adventure or to wreck personal vengeance upon the enemy, (for God says: Dearly beloved, avenge not yourself, but rather give place unto wrath, for it is written: Vengeance is mine, I will repay, said the Lord). But a Christian follows the flag in obedience of God, who sends the soldiers into the field by the ordained and constituted governmental powers for the punishment of the evil doers. Though he shoots and wounds and kills he is by no means a murderer, but a part of the government itself, which beareth not the sword in vain, but is a minister of God. So we see that a Christian can be a soldier with a clear and good conscience before God.[153]

Warns was reminded that his Christian faith would "give him courage in danger, endurance and perseverance even in the jaws of death" and that he should not fear death for "should he be called away by death, because the Lord wills it, he can confidently commend his spirit into the hands of His Savior, who stand ready to receive it." Death on a battle field, Oberheu counseled, "If it be a death in Christ, cannot separate from Christ, but calls a Christian into the immediate, visible fellowship of God." Pastor Oberheu concluded with "this was the essence of my service flag speech. The church was filled."[154]

What would become the final assault on the German lines was planned for 1 November, 1918, and even though the Eighty-ninth had been in continuous action for ten days it would be one of two spearhead divisions for this offensive. At this point the Eighty-ninth Division tried a different strategy:

> The 89th also succeeded in misleading the Germans. Instead of forming assault troops along the obvious jump-off line at the edge of the woods, these experienced leaders placed the men, under the cover of darkness, in the open field in front of the woods. When the Germans concentrated their counter fire on the woods, they missed the infantrymen.[155]

The Eighty-ninth made a five-mile advance by nightfall of 1 November. A member of the nearby Eightieth Division described the devastation: "As we advanced, the roads and fields were strewn with dead Germans, horses, masses of artillery, transports, ammunition limbers, helmets, guns and bayonets." [156] The 355th Infantry took the village of Beaufort at 7:30 AM on 4 November. They had now been at the front for fifteen consecutive days. At 2:00 AM on 11 November, Private Warns crossed the Meuse River near the important steel-manufacturing town of Stenay.[157] An official history of the Eighty-ninth division explained why Stenay, France was a desirable destination: "The Division had been in the line a considerable period without proper bathing facilities and since it was realized that if the enemy were permitted to remain in Stenay, our troops would be deprived of the billets and the probable bathing facilities there", instructions were sent "to push forward directly and take Stenay."[158] In the aftermath of the Meuse-Argonne offensive, speculation that the war might soon be over had permeated the home front, and John's Uncle Jake offered this perspective: "Report has it that the war is about over, last evening's news was the Kaiser had abdicated. Hope it is true and that the world will again enjoy the longed-for peace. What a rejoicing it will be throughout the civilized world."[159] War correspondent Burr Price, upon hearing that an armistice was about to be signed, hurried to the outskirts of Stenay. At six minutes to eleven he heard, "The sound of a gun being fired. I waited for some other gun further away, and waited for the same gun to fire again. But no, it was the last shot. A great silence settled over the hills and valley."[160] Anticipating a spectacle, Captain Eddie Rickenbacker, American flying ace and eventual winner of the Medal of Honor, had taken to the air and later captured the euphoric mood on the Western Front:

> I glanced at my watch. One minute to 11:00, thirty seconds, fifteen. And then it was 11:00 a. m., the eleventh hour of the eleventh day of the eleventh month. I was the only audience for the greatest show ever presented. On both sides of no-man's land, the trenches erupted. Brown-uniformed men poured out of the American trenches, gray-green out of the German. From my observer's seat overhead, I watched them throw their helmets in the air, discard their guns, wave their hands. Then all up and down the front, the two groups of men began edging toward each other across no-man's-land. Seconds before they had been willing to shoot each other; now they came forward. Hesitantly at first, then more quickly, each group approached the other. Suddenly gray uniforms mixed with brown. I could see them hugging each other, dancing, jumping. Americans were passing out cigarettes and chocolate. I flew up to the French sector: There it was even more incredible. After four years of slaughter and hatred, they were not only hugging each other but kissing each other on both cheeks as well.   Star shells, rockets and

flares began to go up, and I turned my ship toward the field. The war was over.[161]

In a hand-written note dated "Early Monday Morning Nov. 11" Warns was ecstatic; "Hurrah! A message brings the news that the armistice was signed all bells are ringing whistles blowing, and shooting going on to beat the band. Rejoicing everywhere. Gott sei Dank [Thank God]. God grant that everything be settled in a hurry now so the world can begin reconstruction work, and may peace reign forever."[162] War Correspondent Burr Price reported that on the evening of 11 November, "Fires are burning tonight along the Meuse front. From dugout, barracks and back camps our American doughboys are sending skyward rockets of triumph, shooting Roman candles and setting off red, white and blue flares. The heavens for miles around are illumined."[163] From San Francisco, Warns' cousin Hattie exclaimed, "well Cousin you boys have fought and licked the 'Hun.' Thank God it is all over. We would all like to see you boys home for xmas but I don't suppose you can all be back this year. I see by the papers that President Wilson is to eat Christmas dinner with the American Troops . . . wish you could see the Frisco shop windows at xmas time John, they are simply gorgeous, there is so much that you can't make up your mind as to what you want."[164] When news of the 11 November armistice officially reached South Dakota, the residents of Wentworth indulged in one final patriotic outburst as the "Kaiser was hung by the neck in the main street of Wentworth until pronounced dead and the remains cremated."[165] Even Warns' nine-year old sister Selma was caught up in the Kaiser-stomping patriotism: "I was up to Rutland this morning I saw the Kaiser and a American cannon, the Kaiser was standing up but he won't stand long when that cannon goes off on him—won't stand he will lay—it was a play toy. I hope it sticks him don't you?" Selma made it clear she wanted direct mail from her big brother: "I might write another letter but next time instead [of] addressing to Dorothy [Dorothea] poot [put] it to me—I told Dimples [Dorothea] that it was for me instead [of] for her."[166]

Private Warns was understandably jubilant in his first letter after November 11th:

Dearest Mother: "It's over—really over" and though I can't understand it I escaped—thanks to the Lord—without getting hurt. We've licked em and we—so far as we know—will soon be on our way home. Anyhow I still figure on Christmas Dinner. Oh I just feel dazed yet. I've tried to write to you every day and although I constantly think of you and home I just couldn't settle down and think clear enough to write. Everything seems so quiet in spite of truck motors and the other noises. I never heard the last shot—was sound asleep—guess I ain't woke up yet. Am inclosing a clipping—we took measurements for new clothes yesterday. This is some jumbled up letter but I can't think and write. The Lord kept me safe and sound and he will sure by prayers all well until we meet—Christmas.[167]

A few days later, having gathered himself, Warns sat down to write a slightly more detailed description of his experiences as the Eighty-ninth Division crossed the Meuse River on 10 November 1918:

Dearest Mother: Just a note to let you know I'm hale and hearty, but still somewhat dazed from this quick turn of events. The two weeks just previous to the armistice were rather tough—can therefore appreciate the present state of affairs so much more. You can't imagine dear mother how different things are now from what they have been. And never will I be able to thank the Lord for protecting and bringing me through to see these days, as I should. I only pray that we may soon be together again. I won't attempt to describe how things were—only that we crossed the famous Meuse the morning of the armistice and though that Meuse may be a famous river, Battle Creek has it skinned all hallow for looks. The towns just this side and on the other side are well preserved and were still occupied by civilians who were mighty glad to see us. We have been issued some new equipment and are drilling so as to get back to shape—Rumors as to when this division returns are numerous and of all description—however we are one of the crack divisions and 85 % farmers, which makes it look as though we will be among the first. I enclose a clipping from S&S I've seen the place from a point about four kilo away and understand (and hope) we are going there—have seen a number of historic towns lately. We have a Y and can purchase tobacco, cigars, cigarettes, candy, etc. Well So long, more later, John

Love to Uncle Henry and others[168]

The Eighty-ninth Division had been at the front for eighty-two days, advanced approximately thirty miles, experienced twenty-eight days in battle, lost 1,466 men in action, had 5,625 wounded, and captured 5,061 German prisoners.[169] General Pershing commended the Eighty-ninth Division for its "splendid accomplishments which will live through all history." He reflected on the last two offensives that brought the conflict to an end by pointing out that after the reduction of the Saint Mihiel Salient, "for more than six weeks, you battered against the pivot of the enemy line of the Western Front" at a position "fortified by four years of labor designed to render it impregnable . . . that position you broke utterly and thereby hastened the collapse of the enemy's military power." He observed that the Eighty-ninth Division would long be remembered for "storming of obstinately defended machine gun nests, your penetration, yard by yard, of woods and ravines, your heroic resistance in the face of counter-attacks supported by powerful artillery fire." Pershing provided additional accolades for the Eighty-ninth, proclaiming that "your achievement, which is scarcely to be equaled in American history, must remain a source of proud satisfaction to the troops who participated in the last campaign of the war."[170]

Private Warns and his 355th Infantry of the Eighty-ninth Division had now played a significant role in the last two major offensives of 1918, offensives which proved decisive in bringing World War One to an end on 11 November, 1918. Warns kept his loved ones as well-informed of his front-line experiences as the vagaries of combat and the censors allowed.

By mid-1918 his references to the Germans as "Huns" indicate that he, as was the case with his sister Anna on the home front, was now under the influence of war-time propaganda. In turn, letters from the home front, especially from his Uncle Jake and pastor Oberhau, sustained Warns by encouraging him to rely on his Christian faith. While it is clear that Private Warns hoped to be home by Christmas, 1918, the Eighty-ninth Division had other plans for Private Warns, who was skilled as a bi-lingual speaker and writer.

CHAPTER FIVE

Occupation

"One sure way of insulting a Saarburger is to be caught drinking water."
- Private John Warns

On 12 November, 1918 Major General Frank L. Winn assumed command of the Eighty-ninth Division which was now head-quartered in Stenay, France. By this time, Warns knew that his hopes for returning to South Dakota in time for Christmas would not be realized because the Eighty-ninth Division would serve as part of an oc-cupying force of around 200,000 American soldiers that began marching into Germany on 24 November.[171] Letters from Private Warns provide us with a rare first-hand look at a neglected aspect of World War One: the 1918-1919 temporary occupation of Germany by American forces. These occupying forces performed numerous post-Armistice duties, including taking possession of German prison camps, confiscating German weap-ons, enforcing sanitary and liquor ordinances, and enforcing regulations that required returning German soldiers to be out of uniform four days after returning home. While the Paris Peace Conference was convening in 1919 to produce what would become the Versailles Peace Treaty, American troops also maintained discipline and training "to keep them in first class fighting trim in case of resumption of hostilities."[172] In order to provide quality opportunities during spare time, the Young Man's

Christian Association (YMCA) organized entertainment, educational and athletic competitions.

On 26 November, 1918 Private Warns wrote from Sapogne, France. Although the French had erected a huge arch of evergreens and allied flags, and bands were playing around the hour, Private Warns was not caught up in the spirit of celebration. Instead he observed how eastern France had been devastated by the war as the civilian poor were coming back to:

> shot up horses and artillery plowed fields—I feel sorry for them—poor old grandmothers—hardly able to walk with heavy packs on their backs. Old men bent over with age and rheumatism, crippled men and young and pretty, but tired looking girls. Little children with hardly clothing enough to cover their legs—hungry looking bunch. The Germans must and will pay for all of this and we stay here until they do.[173]

From Wentworth, Warns' Uncle Jake had asked John "do you see any of the atrocities committed by the Germans? There are some great rumors here, some of which haven't the ring of truth in them, and some so ridiculously unreasonable that I for one absolutely refuse to believe them."[174] Having now entered territory formerly occupied by Germany during the war, Warns was in a position to answer this question and he observed: "Of atrocities such as cutting off children's legs, arms, etc. and committing other horrors that we heard about back home I have not seen—but the natural horrors that follow war are horrors as you wouldn't believe without seeing." As Private Warns concluded this letter he contemplated his homecoming and remarked, "When I get back home there's just two things I want, Mother's cooking and farm work. Say dad you couldn't get me off that there farm with a crowbar—damn this canned stuff and working for a fellow wearing a stiff collar."[175]

By 10 December, 1918 the entire Eight-ninth Division was in Germany and Warns' 355th Infantry was headquartered in Saarburg.[176] The principal activities of the division were railroad guarding and border patrol. Warns' ability to speak German landed him a job as an interpreter, and he often entered German homes to make arrangements for the billeting of American troops. Thus far he had operated as an interpreter in Luxemburg, Esternack, Eisennack, Bitburg, Binsfled, Speicher, Grosslittgen, Wittlich, Friers, Conz and Stenay "and the Lord only knows wherever else." He explained the procedure: "When we move our billeting staff goes ahead in Fords. There are five officers and nine of us interpreters and sergeants and we have four Fords." John's conviction that the upper classes of German society were most responsible for the causes of World War One matched President Wilson's view that a few German militarists had started the war and influenced his approach to billeting: "We pick the finest homes for our quarters and the people treat us to anything the town has. In finding 'quarters' for the boys I always make the rich take the largest number of boys as they are the real cause of the war. The poor I let off as easy as possible." Warns made it clear that while he had hoped to be home for Christmas, he certainly could not complain about his current situation: "In fact I wish you all could celebrate here with me. The folks we are staying with are well-to-do wine growers—they make from 8-11 fuder of wine each year and a fuder is worth from 800-1200 mark. One sure way of insulting a Saarburger is to be caught drinking water."[177]

He continued by pointing out that the "host" family had won awards in Chicago and St. Louis for their wine-making, and after drinking a glass of "82" made this observation: "Dear folks, if wine like that could be had at home instead of rotten whiskies there never would be any prohibition talk. One enjoys wines here for they do not make one dizzy or give you a headache the morning after." John had come to appreciate the status of wine in German cuisine: "We have wine with our meals—wine in-between—and its old wine, rich and mellow—never had anything like it at home." Even though John was grateful to be experiencing some of the more refined aspects of German life, his duties as an interpreter also brought him face-to-face with the war's impact on Germans:

> In my line of duty I enter from 50 to 200 houses at every
> place we go and you can't imagine how homesick I get
> when I see kids of Sally's and Dot's age—thin and hollow

cheeked and a lost, forlorn look in their eyes. Your kids there sure have it good and you always want to remember it. I didn't know how good I had it either, until I hit France. But the Lord was mighty good to me, and every time I enter a house where a son is still among the missing or is a useless cripple for life—and both cases are oh, so frequent here—I am reminded of God's wonderful mercy. And I try to be thankful, too.[178]

"Saarburg, Germany"

Christmas Day 1918 was not a joyful occasion for Anna. She managed to isolate herself in a quiet corner of the Warns home to write a poignant seven-page letter, detailing what each family member had given and received as gifts. From the following excerpts it is clear that John's absence weighed heavily on her mind, that the flu epidemic was impacting Wentworth's social fabric, and that Saint Peter's Lutheran Church had dropped German language services. American involvement in World War I had accelerated the Americanization of "German" Americans:

Well dear I do hope you've had a Merry Christmas. Sometimes I wonder how Christmas can be merry this year. How scattered our "bunch" is. How scattered all over the whole world and yet, in a way nearer than ever. In a way I should be the happiest creature alive and yet I ain't. My heart has been so close to my mouth all day that I've been afraid to open my mouth. Well maybe I'll have reason to be truly happy real soon. I hope so. Now for "our" Christmas. I decorated the room and the tree as usual except that I put the large Xmas wreath around our beloved service flag. The children were of course quite delighted, but I believe we all felt the absence of some important factor. I wanted a letter from you so bad today, but none came. Don't see why you don't write. We've only received one letter since Nov. 11 and that dated Nov. 15th. The program (Christmas) was all in American, and not as good as usual as they didn't have much time to practice because of the "flu".[179] Will have a party either Sunday or New Year. Better come over for it. I shouldn't enjoy it much but must do something to get the "discontent" and "longing" out of my system. Well so much of myself. Wish I were in a happier state of mind but alas, how am I to be. There is no place like home quite as lonesome as home when they aren't all home. Well so long kid, do wish you'd write. Am just dying by inches to hear from you.[180]

In a letter Warns wrote just after Christmas he sent home pictures of himself and asked, "Do I look natural? I am putting on fat again now—my blouse is so tight I could bust off the buttons by taking a deep breath. It sure is comfortable and easy living here and were it not for getting home-sick I would as soon stay a while." This was too much for his sister Anna and she fired back, giving John a hard time about his gaining weight (he later admitted that he had gained thirty pounds during the occupation): "Say why don't you get your picture taken now in Germany? Ma wants to know if you are so big that you can't get on a picture any more", and "Say I'd rather you'd talk a little less about that darn wine, don't you know that we can't get any here and besides Mamma worries because she's afraid you drink too much."[181]

"Private John Warns in Germany"

Warns had received a Christmas packet from home and reported that "the homemade candy sure was great" and he appreciated the "deck of cards." Warns told Anna "I still carry the bible Verein sent me and as it is smaller will keep carrying it," but what he enjoyed the most "were the three cigars—we can buy them here—mark apiece—but it's been a long time since I've smoked a real U. S. cigar." Next he made a request: "Say sis take a picture of the biggest hog on the farm and also of a good heap of good corn—I would like to show the people here what a hog looks like back in the states and also what corns is." In closing he wrote: "Well I'll have to quit. Kiss mother and greet all the rest for me. Uncle Jake wrote that Dad had a splendid lot of seed corn and I see that Dad's hogs are selling for $75 to NP [Nonpartisan League] members—do ask if nonmembers can buy at the same price—haha. See Bates got beat and feel sorry—wonder whether my vote ever got back." As a postscript he added, "We may be home in time to celebrate the fourth."[182] In another letter Uncle Jake wrote to say "I learned from Anne [Anna] that you are in Germany. Oh boy, but you are lucky." And he offered this perspective from the home front: "Christmas was sad very sad for many families in the U. S. for thousands and thousands of mostly young men and women were victims of flu." The epidemic had reached Wentworth, where "owing to the flu epidemic there is no school . . . . Everything is dead like, meetings of all kind were poorly attended, even dances, because people are afraid."[183]

On 4 January, 1919 Warns wrote a short letter home "to let you know that I'm hale and hearty." He speculated about the future: "Everything indicates that we are to stay here until peace is signed." Saarburg's Old-World charms were no substitute for spending Christmas at home: "it's only the lonesomeness and longing for home that makes staying here a drudge instead of a pleasure."[184] Uncle Jake offered encouragement: "Am glad you were so fortunate as to be stationed in such a wonderful beautiful place. Sure, time must not seem long in a place like that. You sure are lucky." Attempting to get Warns to look on the bright side, he wrote, "Why boy, lots of American tourists pay stacks of money to go to such places to see the sights." Uncle Jake went on to exhort Warns to avoid the pitfalls of revenge and instead practice the Golden Rule:

> Well I am glad you are well and thank God with you who so mercifully watched over and brought you through this terrible conflict unharmed while thousands of others to your right and left fell dead, or were crippled for life. And as God has been merciful and kind to you, so I hope you will also be merciful and kind to those who were our enemies, the German people.[185]

Anna's melancholic Christmas letter prompted John to respond in a deeply introspective manner. He contended that his ninety days on the Western Front had transformed him: "If the days I've spent under shell fire are dreams, they are nothing of the dreams of the days before April 27th." Wondering about adjusting to life after the war he remarked, "When I look over the past I feel that I never will be able to readjust myself to the life as it used to be before the war." He expressed regret about parts of his past and suggested he had learned some life-changing lessons, "When I think of the foolish days spent foolishly—time and energy wasted. Acts unworthy, the careless life I led. When I think of these I'm always thankful that I was permitted to go through the little hell I went through and come out of—perhaps physically not quite as healthy, but a dam site more of a man." John told Anna that his Christmas had been different as well: "I too spent my Christmas mostly in thinking—and looking forward to another Christmas." He had attended a Lutheran service on Christmas morning and "in the evening a beautiful service in the Catholic Church." Reflecting on his duties as an interpreter, John told Anna he had been in "every house" in Saarburg and "in every room in every house", engaged in work he described as "amusing, interesting and instructive." He regretted that "duty" caused him to act "disinterested and seemingly hard", but he reminded Anna that he had only recently been waging war against the German people: "Then I remember the days of St. Mihial [Mihiel] and Romagne and again the unforgettable days at Beaufort and—don't think I'm revengeful or hard-hearted—but one who hasn't been there can't understand." However, he was grateful that "the Germans do all they can to make things comfortable for us as a rule—we have the best each home has to offer." His living quarters included "a beautiful featherbed—electric lighted room— private bath and the people do everything to show me that I'm welcome." John described a niece who was visiting his host family as "a real German lass in notions," and he told Anna that "once in a while I chat a few moments with her. She's very anxious to learn more about Americans as are all the girls—and I'm in a no-tion they intend to run a race with you American girls for husbands—doubt however if they have more than a ghost of a chance for we are all longing for the girl we can say kiddo to." He did admit that at times there was tension: "It's rather hard at times to keep from talking and joshing with them—but it only needs a thought like 'her father was at Romagne'—the poor girls notice it and really can't or should not be blamed—but it's hard to forget." The YMCA was providing entertainment for the 355th Infantry, and Warns noted that "we also have History, French and German classes."[186] From the home front, Anna wrote to comment on pictures Warns had sent home: "Got your pictures yesterday and sure were delighted. Are you still so fleshy?" She explained that "at first I thought the one where you have your hat on was best but on second thought decided that the one with your cap is prettiest, that is more natural, however both are good and we sure were glad to get them." The family had had a surprise birthday party for "Dimples", who had turned thirteen, and Anna and some friends had gathered at a neighbor's farm to listen to music: "we heard some dandy music. Walter (John's younger brother) has a new piece for ours too, 'Over There' and 'I May Be Gone For a Long Long Time.' Both are pretty and 'Over There' sure is a dandy."[187]

"Walter Warns"

On the back of this photo, which includes the farm house in the background, younger brother Walter wrote, "Der Bro, I shot this rabbit and skinned it. It weighed 8 lbs. We ate the meat and I sold the skin for 20 cents."

"Private John Warns poses for a photo in the American occupied zone of post-World War One Germany."

By 1 February, 1919 Private Warns described how he had become more of a wine connoisseur, but claimed he still preferred homemade ice cream:

> The Burger miester opened his heart and got out a bottle of Jungfer wine-which means the first crop of a wine berry-of 1914. A really rare wine and of a delicious taste, next came a 1914 Wagner and then a 1910 Rheinart. Which with 2 good German cigars-not the cabbage sort-helped greatly towards my enjoying the eve.

> I wish Daddy could enjoy a bottle each night. If he were a Lt or Captain he might be-ha-ha. Well all the wine in the Saarburger cellars ain't worth a dish of homemade ice cream.[188]

Cousin Hattie anticipated the advent of Prohibition, which became a reality one year later with the Eighteenth Amendment to the U. S. Constitution, with this advice: "Say Cousin [of] mine don't get to use to drinking German wines as you may go thirsty when you get back as we have a very bright outlook for a dry U. S. A. hooray."[189]

On 18 February, 1919 Warns re-started a pocket diary after pointing out that he had lost three diaries already.[190] In his 21 February, 1919 entry he refers to the 19 February, 1919 assassination attempt on French Prime Minister Clemenceau, who was currently representing France at the Paris Peace conference: "Just learned that Clemenceau was shot on the 20 [19th]—does not seem to cause much feeling among the Germans—last reports he is still living." Warns believed that given the troubled post-war situation in Europe, it was important that Clemenceau survive: "Hope he pulls through as France cannot afford to lose him. Battles in Poland continue, also strikes along the Rhine."[191] An anarchist named Emile Cottin, had fired seven shots into the car in which Clemenceau was riding, one of which struck Clemenceau in the back. Clemenceau did survive and later joked that Cottin should, "be locked up for eight years, with intensive training in a shooting gallery."[192]

Resuming his correspondence with Anna, Warns described rambunctious drives through German villages and expressed his hope that he would be home by June, 1919:

By the way we laughed until our sides ached coming home. We would go through these little villages at about 30 per and the mud and water would splash 15-20 feet on each side—every time we passed a civilian he would stop and carefully brush his clothes, and the girls and women———would lift their skirts over their heads and sometimes they didn't wear underskirts—I'll bet they cussed. Oh—I wasn't going to forget. The battle we fought was a divisional maneuver and the entire Division took part. Sure was a fine sight.

Our last dope is that we leave here Feb last and get in the states June 1st—But don't stop writing.[193]

"Private John Warns confessed in a letter to his sister Anna that he had taken wild car rides through German villages."

In an eleven-page letter to Anna on 2 March, 1918, Warns told "Tommy" [Anna] he had been acquiring some souvenirs from a "shell shocked" survivor of the war, and he made reference to a bloody battle:

The bracelets are from near Gesnes-Gesnes, the place where we got the German machine guns—some three hundred machine guns. Had them made into bracelets at Trier by a fellow who got gassed and shell shocked. When I handed them to him he was shaking like a leaf and would twitch all over. Oh God but war sure leaves awful cripples.

Sent a box the other day with a German Reserve Canteen, which will make a pretty remembrance hanging on the wall—the man that owned it was executed in France as a spy.

It shows just about where the 32nd got hell—one of the bloodiest battles of the war was fought on these grounds-the dead humans were so thick that they were piled up for barricades against machine gun bullets. We lost over a thousand men on this front. [194]

At this point Warns made some intriguing comments about his connection to the Nonpartisan League and his evolving political perspective, indicating that Theodore Roosevelt's attempt to link the NPL with Lenin, Trotsky and the Bolsheviks had reached the troops in Europe: "Hope I got NP [NPL] papers. Have heard a lot of the NP lately-It has been intimated that they were connected with the Russian Bolsheviks but at any rate from what little information we get I'm afraid Socialism will get an awful hold in the states." John was still intrigued by the possibility that the NPL could offer viable alternatives to the two-party political system and capitalism, and he continued, "In discussion of the pro and cons with others but at heart I am mighty near a Socialist myself. And I can honestly say that 60-80 percent of the boys that seen the front will at a later day worry our capitalists and politicians like hell."[195]

By 4 March, 1919 Warns had reached the Rhine River. In this letter to Anna he described a church he had visited, and a story he had been told about a medieval injustice reminded him of the "food kings" that the Nonpartisan League was challenging in the United States:

Then went down to see the Rhine. Some creek—but take the legends castles and forts away and there wouldn't really be much left. With all formalities we both spit in the river and then took some good views of it. The pictures are to be ready Thursday eve.

Walked the beautiful promenade and avenues, looked over the old Roman forts and also Erhenbreitstein—a fort that could never be taken without artillery. It stands about half a mile over the river and its walls range from four to forty feet in thickness...

The interior of the church impressed one as though it really was sacred, a feeling that many churches cannot make you feel. We stayed there about a half hour just sitting and thinking. Then we went to the pier and got on our boat, we left at ten and upstream enjoyed music and lectures on the old castles and fortresses, the first worth mentioning in Stolsenfels which belonged to the exkeiser [ex-Kaiser] a palest [palace] like they are not and I sincerely hope never will be in the states. The two burgs of the enemy brothers with the wall between them, the mouse thrum where the old count had his grain stored and in a dry year the people come up and begged for food—he led them into a big barn with the promise to give them food, when they were all in he had fire set to the building and as they burned he laughed over their shrieks and said "Listen to the mice Squeal" that night mice overrun his burg, in desperation he went over to a tower on an island in the river just below the burg, the mice swam the thirty foot of water and followed him and he was eaten alive before morning. **Lord how I wish the mice would get busy with some of our food kings back home.** There are about thirty different castles and forts along the 49 kilos we made and the only other one I can just remember the legend of is the one where the king of Hessen lived who made the deal with King George

71

of England whereby the Hessen troops were sent across to fight us in the revolutionary war. The contract was signed in the self-same castle. And it's the only castle along the Rhine that has never been destroyed at one time or other. I'm sending a bunch of cards of all the places I've seen and will tell you more about them in JULY.[196]

When John learned that some of his letters home had been published in local and regional newspapers, including the *Sioux Falls Argus Leader* and the *Madison Sentinel*, he warned that if any more were published he would quit writing: "When I got there he showed me part of one of my letters which had been published in the *Argus*, and last night I got the roll of papers and found another letter in the *Sentinel*. Now if you insist on publishing my letters I'll have to quit writing. There's no one there who reads the papers that Id care to have read word from me at all."[197] Apparently this request from Warns in March, 1918 was ignored by his family, and they proceeded to send John's letters to the *Sioux City Journal*, which prompted John to write in September, 1918: "Would mention, while I think of it that, they having been printed—you would send me the letters the "*Sentinel*" printed and I understand the *Sioux City Journal* also published one. If you have it I sure would like to see it— but please- dear folks—don't let any more get in the printer's hands. They can get their letters from better writers and I don't like at all the idea of having strangers read my letters—and besides it's strictly against rules and regulations."[198]

When the United States entered World War One against Germany in April of 1917, it aligned itself with England and France on the Western Front, and Russia on the Eastern Front. In October of 1917 Lenin, Trotsky and the Bolsheviks had gained control of the Russian government, and with the Treaty of Brest-Litovsk on 3 March, 1918 they had negotiated Russia out of the Great War.[199] By 1919 the Bolsheviks, known as the Reds, were engaged in a gruesome civil war against a coalition of opposition forces known as the Whites. Warns appears to make a reference to this series of events in Russia: "Everything is quiet here and there is no chance of anything starting but over in the east things are pretty wild. Our government made I believe a sad mistake by ever agreeing with that eastern bunch. If we would have told 'em to behave or we would come over—they'd have behaved." And in this letter he also makes it clear that he will not be home until July, 1919: "Well Tommy dear. I guess we won't be home before July 4th so that means a long while yet. Hope everybody's well and OK. Tell Dad and the kids hello from me. And write until I get there."[200]

In his 6 March, 1919 diary entry, Warns described meeting a couple of truck drivers who had arrived from Paris: "They seen Wilson's entrance into Paris, also was at Paris when the armistice was signed." Warns was intrigued; "the stories of Paris life as they tell it is rather interesting." He was most interested to learn that the "fliers would—if they were able to—make one trip a week to the front and celebrate the other six." He wondered if the one day a week fighter pilot's schedule had deprived soldiers like himself of the support they could have used on the front lines: "this might account for the scarcity of our planes every time one of the Dutch come over." Warns' 7 March, 1919 diary entry detailed an encounter with a "shell-shocked" German veteran "who made the Belgium drive and probably has a lot on his conscience. Came back demented." Warns described him as "perfectly harmless during the day but imagines the French are after him nights." Warns did not admire the manner in which this veteran was being treated: "His father put him under lock and key without light and there he raves all night long." When Warns asked the veteran's father "why they didn't turn on the light," the father's response was "he should get over his craziness." Warns surmised that this regrettable situation was related to the German class structure: "That's the type of the lower class here—they expect to be treated as a dog—if you treat them better they presume you are afraid of them." To Warns there was a lesson to be learned: "That's what class distinction brings—may we never have it in the states."[201]

Writing again from Saarburg, Germany, John told Anna more about the Wagner's wine business:

> We learned about the methods used in selling wines—Mr Wagner has some 25 men on his staff who purchase wine drink wine and otherwise do nothing. Four of these men are in the states two in Calif and one in Kentucky—I never knew that wine was made in Kentucky but here Southern US wines are quite famous here.

What they say about not getting headaches from Saarwines is bosh. By George there's six of us that can prove it. Otherwise I am hale and hearty and busy. And homesick. And swearing because you don't write, Well it's time for dinner.[202]

"Private John Warns enjoys a glass of fine Saarburg wine."

In early April 1919, Private Warns took a trip to Paris: "Left here Friday morning at 6:30 and got into Trier at 9. Left there at 4:30 in the afternoon and got into Paris the next afternoon." On his way back to Germany, Warns witnessed the after-math of the war's destruction and offered this description:

The old war grounds sure look a fright—for miles and miles one cannot find a space a yard wide where a shell hasn't exploded—I'm sending a few cards but they are really mild. I seen old women and little children—families of 6-12 all living in cellars or dug outs or a room in the house that possibly wasn't entirely destroyed. The people there are all shell shocked and are half-witted.—It's awful. And these parts only seen 2 years of the war—how must it look around Flanders where they had four years of it. The butcher asked us with tears in his eyes not to bury animals that had the glanders or died of old age—How would you like to be a poor dutchman?

In this letter John made another reference to the post-war political turmoil: "there's an awful feeling of unrest especially among the lower class," and in contrast to his earlier statement that he would probably be a Socialist after the war, in this instance he appears to express ambivalence toward Socialism: "About 50 kilos from here they are striking, and social-ists are gaining ground—The east looks rather fierce. We still have men fighting and they are having a regular war there. The only way to end it is to feed the poor and hang the agitators."[203]

Back in Saarburg, Private Warns used a typewriter to write a lengthy letter to Anna on 7 April, 1918 as he returned to the theme of the superi-ority of German wine:

> The caretaker mentioned that there was a good cellar and of course we gave him to understand that we had seen such cellars as Rhinerts, Grims, Wagners, etc. at Saarburg and we didn't think there could be any better on this side of the Rhine. Oh but we were altogether wrong we were told and even Wagner could not show wines like his lordship had them. We were interested and told him that we would be pleased to be shown. He did. I thought I had seen wine cellars but I guess I hadn't started. Wagner without a doubt has the most modern cellar around, This cellar is not modern-some parts are three hundred years old, but the I've not seen the mammoth cave I reckon it hasn't much on these cellars. And Tommy! such wine——We sampled some nine or ten different kinds all 15ner or older and of the finest grades grown in the area. I seen probably 300 fuders of 100 liters each and I didn't see a tenth of the cellar. The wines here are the kind that one gets in cafes with tinfoil corks and gold monogram seals and he showed us the price list where we seen to our

surprise that these wines sold over the counter for from twenty to thirty marks a bottle, at that rate I get away with a hundred marks of wine and I RODE THAT WHEEL HOME. Really you all can't understand what this Saar white wine is, it cannot be compared in any way with the wines I ever drank at home. Virginia Dare is in comparison that poorest wine I've drank.[204] If only I could take home a case with me for Dad and the rest of you. I did make arrangements for future possibilities.[205]

Going into World War One, Warns had been a Prohibition supporter, but all of the exposure to fine German wines appears to have caused Warns to reverse his earlier position, and he now warned that he and his fellow veterans would wage a militant attack if Prohibition was in place upon their return:

The states may be dry when we get back-but we learned how to fight the enemies of liberty here and we won't have a hell of a hard time finishing the job there. It would sure make those sneaking politicians who put over this dirty deal behind our back, wish they were in a concrete dugout if they knew what we intend to do with em. We understand that the feminine trouser wearers and the spinsters were shocked when they learned that the boys used cigarettes while facing death on the front line, without a doubt all those that got killed with a cigarette in their mouth or in their jeans went straight to hell. They would have went there anywhere if they would have been allowed to decide between a country run by those umbrella sticks and hades.[206]

It is also clear that Private Warns was troubled by the post-war arrival of wealthy Americans in Europe who had avoided going to a war that had been waged by the "common class" of Americans:

The papers say that a goodly share of the fellows who got exemptions on account of their personality and fear of getting tanned or abused are coming over now to see the historic grounds the common class fought and died on, now this would be great if we could only get back in time to make a law prohibiting their return. I've seen some of them myself—leather trunks-pajamas-wardrobes and all. They come well protected in an enclosed car and they expect colonels to kneel at their mercy as for a buck private, guess they don't know there's such a thing in the army. Here we're are trying to show the Germans what a democratic people are like and somebody permits these superhumans to run around loose and spoil it all. Well so much for cussing this time.[207]

John was convinced that space that should have been used to transport letters to soldiers, was instead occupied with the accoutrements of the wealthy. The months of occupation were wearing down John's patience:

I spoke of not getting any mail, tonight nine letters get in for the company-of course we oughtened holler, we realize that all these politicians-prohibitionist-YMCA men-profiteers and sightseers have to get over and all available boat space is needed for the two dozen odd suitcases trunks and wardrobes each brings over with him, needed to make life livable and show the Huns what a gentleman should have in the lines of cloths to appear respectable come first. But we ought to have mail once in a while say every month or so. Damn it we have that much coming for being soldiers.[208]

Frustrated soldiers of the occupation had found creative ways to express their emotions: "The newest piece of music here sung to the tune of The Star Spangled Banner begins like this: We come over to fight, and not to roam. So why in hell don't they send us home. And the newest piece of news just off the bulletin board is that the 314th engineers are building an old soldiers home at Treves for the 89th."[209] Even the arrival of spring and Easter did not steer John's thoughts away from the drudgery of being a part of the occupying forces:

> The weather is just wonderful. The first trees are all blooming and the hillsides are just covered with corn flowers and other wild flowers. Today the second shipment of American food for the Germans arrived and the civilians are just wild. It's been holiday for the Germans ever since Thursday morning. Somehow I haven't the Easter spirit at all. I just can't command my thots on Easter—it seems like any other day—nothing to think— to plan—do what you are told and no more—it makes a fellow dependent. Oh how I long for the day when I can say "I'm free".[210]

John offered these observations about the situation in Europe: "Europe is sure some theater stage. In a piece of land a little bigger than Texas they have peace conferences, Art exhibitions, Republic Government, war strikes, plagues, murders and high life. Yesterday's casualties in the strike regions—about 50 klm from here, they have about 200 dead and several hundred wounded, in Posen [Poznan] Polen [Poland] and Archangel the war goes merrily on." Even though John had specific dates to report concerning his departure from Europe, his combat and occupational experiences had definitely tempered his enthusiasm: "Our sailing dates are Leave Saarburg May 6th—leave either Brest or Amsterdam May 16th, mustered out June 1st." He noticed that the prospect of an imminent return to the United States had generated a degree of introspection: "Don't you know, now that it's a fact and settled nobody seems to be hilarious—we are all thinking deeply about the future." His thoughts transitioned to the potential for political upheaval in the United States: "We have seen enough here to make us realize that the states are about due for a crisis. And that we have a hard fight ahead of us."[211]

Five days later, John pondered just what exactly a return to civilian life would be like: "Oh I just can't express the sensation of knowing that within a few weeks I'll be back on the farm. I wonder how things will seem to me, wonder if I'll be surprised at the new America." He expressed doubts about making the transition from the intensity of the Western Front to rural life in South Dakota, "Wonder if I'll like the new style of doing things—wonder if I can feel satisfied with common everyday life." Would he be able to "forget what I want to forget and remember what I want to remember of the past year?" He knew that his days of drinking fine German wine were coming to an end and asked himself "wonder if I can stand it without a drink." Even his clothing would change: "Wonder how long trousers will feel—Oh hell what's the use of wondering."[212]

From Warns' diary entries in early May, 1919, it is clear that while the U. S. army occupation of post-war Germany had created some tensions between the Germans and the American soldiers, certain bonds of affection had also developed. As the Eighty-ninth Division began to depart from Saarburg, Warns noted that "everybody is celebrating this evening—at the park the Band played for 15 minutes and a fourth of Saarburg was there. The boys were showered with flowers and many a tear dimmed eye tried to hide itself in the crowd." By 9 May, 1919 Warns reported the: "town is as quiet as death. They left at 6 this morning and even at this early hour the park was crowded—now there are less than a dozen 89th soldiers and officers in town. Everywhere I go I must drink a glass of wine and say farewell and I drank my share before breakfast."[213] Warns was one of the last Americans to leave Saarburg, Germany.

In one of his last letters from Europe, Private Warns put pen to paper from Paris on Mother's Day, and crafted this tribute to Dora:

> Dear Mother:- Today is Mother's day again:- only a year mother dear since I wrote the last mother's day letter- But what a year! ... Soon – just about 3 more weeks- we will celebrate a real mother's day but today I must tell you mother dear that it was memories of you that made training easy and endurable, memories of you that gave me backbone and courage when we went up to the front, memories of you that made it possible to face hell itself and your prayers that made it possible for me to come through this hell nearly without a scratch. And after the armistice it was again you mother who has kept me on

the straight and narrow path as much as a human being can. I can't never begin to thank you and I'm not going to try. But when I have returned I will show my appreciation to the best mother in the world. As things have changed there so have I changed, all of us who faced powder and smoke have but I'm sure mother you have a son with whom you can be satisfied. He has learned much and has grown 20 years older in thoughts and habit. He sure has seen 20 years go by in 12 short months. We leave Paris tonight at 7:00 for Brest where we return to our outfits. We left Saarburg two days after the troops left. It sure was quiet there. There were about 5 or 6 officers and a dozen men left, where 2 days before there were 3,000 men and officers. We had a wonderful and enjoyable time before we left, was showered with flowers. Had to drink a wine in every house I entered and most families insisted on sending a bottle along. I usually refused but I did have 8 bottles along the way.[214]

"Dora, John's mother, reads a letter from John while sitting on the steps of the Warns farm house."

Warns reached the French coastal city of Brest on 15 May, 1919 and sailed for New York on what he referred to as "sure is some boat."[215]

"Private John Warns on his return to the United States in 1919."

Private Warns was in New York City the weekend of 23 May to 25 May, 1919, and a survey of the New York Times over that weekend serves as a reminder that post-war Europe was mired in social and political upheaval, and it illustrates that New York City, on the doorstep of the Roaring Twenties, was a very different place than Wentworth, South Dakota, situated in the farmland of the Great Plains. Over that weekend the New York Times included a story about 500,000 people marching in the streets of Berlin, Germany, demanding that the German government sign the Treaty of Versailles as they shouted "Let us have peace! We want bread, not bullets." The editorial slant of the New York Times was decidedly anti-Bolshevik and the public was invited to an address entitled "Bulwarks Against Bolshevism" at Carnegie Hall. The U. S. Senate was demanding that the Treaty of Versailles be made public amidst a rancorous debate in which Republican opposition to the treaty was referred to as "perverse." American war hero Alvin York, who killed twenty-five Germans and captured one-hundred and thirty-two in the Argonne, was being honored at a dinner at the Waldorf-Astoria. The Cunard Anchor steamship line offered voyages from New York to Liverpool on six different ocean liners and Best & Company was selling men's suits from $35 to $65, and women's suits from $29.50 to $45.00. The New York Giants were in first place in the National League, the Brooklyn Dodgers were in third place, and the New York Yankees were in third place in the American League. At Loew's Metropolitan Theater, Mary Pickford was starring in the silent comedy-drama movie *Daddy Long Legs*.[216] Warns' final letter to Anna provided details about life in New York City from the perspective of a South Dakota farm boy who now had some travel experience under his belt: "New York is sure a funny town and about as un-American as I could think of anything being." He determined that a lot of New Yorkers were pretentious: "The upper class tries to appear Parisian or Londonarized and the underclass is nothing but foreigners—In Paris I liked the Parisian ways—for they were real. Here it looks like imitation and that's all it is." He was somewhat shocked by the cost of living: "And a soldier is about as much as a tramp here—unless he has beaucoup dough. I paid 65 cents for a couple of eggs, a stack of cakes and a glass of milk. I got my hair cut, a shave and a massage relieved me of 2 bucks—I went into a cigar store and seeing my favorite cigar "Roitan" asked for a couple—They were to be 10 cents straight—40 cents please—Well I ought to have backed out but I didn't—it was a big place and there was a big corral. My room cost me 3 bucks, dinner—it was good—85 cents and supper 65 cents, Ice cream costs 18 cents. There's some kind of tax on it." However, Warns was most disturbed by those who tried to take advantage of him on the streets: "Well all of these things wouldn't hurt so bad, —but them fellows with tin pins—postcard sets and everything in the line of graft just a laying for a fellow. It's a damn right shame—In Germany they didn't dare rob us."[217]

Warns could hardly contain his enthusiasm as he recorded his homeward trek: "Mississippi River at 7:20, in God's country once more. Woke up at 5:30 to find that we were at camp. Never rolled pack so fast in my life. At 5:30 in the evening we were free men. At 6 I was in Des Moines—got out at 1:30. Got a real feast at Sioux City. I'm in S. Dak at last."[218] Warns' pocket diary concludes with ninety signatures that he had gathered during the occupation of Germany and his trip home—friendships forged by the intense camaraderie experienced in World War One. As each one of them signed his name and address they knew that they were the survivors, they had futures. They were home.

CHAPTER SIX

Reconciliation

"If Dad were alive today, he would approve of the use of his story."
-Marvin Warns, 2005

P rivate Warns returned to South Dakota in June, 1919 and worked on the family farm for two years. In 1920 he was employed as the editor of the *Lake County News*, returning to the kind of work he had been exposed to during his youth.[219] From 1922 to 1924 he leased the *Lake County News* and published it. On 1 April, 1924, despite his wartime claim that he was not a good writer, he launched his own newspaper, the *Wentworth Progress*.[220] John married Ida Rottluf of Oldham, South Dakota in 1927, and they had seven children. He remained in the newspaper business until 1938, when he started working a variety of jobs that included an insurance business, income tax service work and managing a telephone company. Between 1936 and 1941 John Warns worked on the "South Dakota Writer's Project", which was funded by the Work's Progress Association of the New Deal. In this capacity he compiled four volumes of Lake County history as he conducted research on all the old newspapers available. His work on this project also took him to the Pettigrew Museum in Sioux Falls and General Beadle College where he reviewed the files of the *Madison Sentinel* and the *Madison Daily Leader*.[221] Beginning in 1941, Warns was involved "with a large commercial gardening venture." His children "all worked together with him and Mother, the venture paid off, it provided food for the family and paid the bills."[222] He attended reunions of the 355th Infantry Association in 1937 (North Platte, Nebraska) and 1938 (Hastings, Nebraska).

"John Warns, editor of the *Wentworth Progress*"

During his time with the American occupation forces in Saarburg, Germany, Warns met the Kaiser family, and just before Warns departed from Saarburg in 1919, Anna Kaiser placed her signature in Warns' *Pocket Diary*. In 1947 Warns, who had generally enjoyed interacting with German people during the 1919 occupation and held no long-term grudges against Germans, reached out to the Kaiser family via the mail, and they responded in a series of six letters, revealing details about the difficulties of life in post-World-War II Germany, and their gratitude for the parcels that Warns sent their way.

Writing from Kassel, Germany, in the American zone of a divided Germany, Mathilde Kaiser told Warns, "You cannot imagine the deep joy your letter made to me and the [to] mine. Your Christmas parcel did not yet arrive and so we have something we shall be glad of." Even though World War II had been over for almost three years, the German people were still suffering, as Mathilde pointed out that "the years after

World War II were so much like the years 1918/19 and reminded me of so many things." Mathilde described for Warns the dilemma she faced in 1945 when her son, Otto returned from captivity and she "had to establish my own household and this was very difficult as I had no food stock." "Bad misery" was avoided that winter when a "kindly American" showed them a "falling-off place, where he had thrown American food-stocks without spoiling them as it was his orders." Another American helped them "by giving us cigarettes, those we exchanged for vegetables and potatoes." She reported that Kassel "is 90% destroyed by air-raids," and that her son Otto and her daughter's fiancé Klaus were now about six feet tall, but "as we lost all clothing and since 1944 you cannot buy anything in Germany, you can imagine that they nearly have nothing to dress [wear]." Their living quarters were Spartan-like as they were only able to "furniture [furnish] indigently as you now cannot buy furniture nor wood in Germany."[223] As late as 1947 residents of the American zone of Germany were still living on rations, as Mathilde reported that "for a week one person gets on the ration card: 5 pounds of dark rye-bread, 4 pounds of potatoes (including the rotten)," and "good vegetables like beans, cauliflower, Brussels sprouts, cucumbers, tomatoes or fruits we have not seen since years. Since 1945 we eat by day: bread—3 slices for breakfast, watery soup for dinner and for supper we eat potatoes and veg-etables." They were exchanging their cigarette rations for "turnips, carrots or beet-roots."[224] In 1947 Otto and her Klaus rode their bicycles to villages and "asked farmers for potatoes in every house as they repaired radios, watches and spectacles and got potatoes for payment. So we have some 100 pounds more than we ought to have and I would not know what to do without them."[225] Personal hygiene was also problematic because "every three months we get a little cake of bad soap," and heating the apartment also presented a challenge because "we get nearly no fuel and often we have to go to the woods and look for twigs and pine cones." Despite the multitude of hardships, Mathilde told Warns: "But, in spite of all misery and sorrow, I have not lost the hope for better times and remember always that sunshine comes after a storm. We often wander and make excursions (Kassal has a wonderful surrounding of hills and woods), thinking: it may cost calories but it is tonic. We enjoy nature, that no one can take [from] us and we sing and have good humor."[226]

Mathilde closed her letter by saying "I have asked you to help us in our momentary need so it happened with the hope that I can thank you one day with typical German products or with a case of good 'Saarwein' that, I hope, you remember well. And have you the same good Schnapps we have at Saarburg?" She promised to send John articles from German newspapers about conditions and social life and then noted that as late as 1948 the flow of information out of Germany was controlled: "I hope they will pass through censorship."[227]

Otto wrote to Warns: "I would like to correspond with one of your children. Is there one who would like to write me?" Otto offered a short summary of his life, explaining that he had been born in Saarburg on 23 August, 1927. During his "nice and happy childhood" he became a member of the Hitler Youth in 1937. At gliding camps Otto "saw the beauty of my German country and became a passionate glider. By all these nice things I had there and the good comrades, I was convinced of the good will of [the] Nazi party." In 1943 he "was enlisted to the Flak-aid corps of German pupils and was stationed at Frankfurt and Trier." In 1945 he was ordered to the Luftwaffe "and so I became an American POW in Germany." Otto's captivity was a harrowing ordeal as it "began with complete plundering (watches, rings, shoes, pullovers and so on)." One of his comrades was shot in reappraisal for a shot he had fired just before being captured, and Otto feared he might be shot as well, but was spared through "the interference of an American officer." Otto claimed that as POWs they "got nearly nothing to eat, 25% of my fellow-sufferers starved, looking through the barbed wire where the food rests of the American kitchen were brought in tubs and spoiled." Then, in addition to this physical suffering "came the sorrow about our relatives, the German defeat and the loss of all we had trusted in. I returned home in rags, looking like a skeleton and hungry as a wolf." But Otto added, he still had his health and "good humor" and was now "rich in experience and practical wisdom." Otto was now an "eye-optician-apprentice" and would finish his training in October, 1948. He was a young man living in fear of the emerging Cold War and his plans were "to emigrate as soon as possible for here the econom-ical condition is bad and there is no hope for turning it better as long as Germany is splitted [split] in eastern and western zones and it may be that Communism will turn it worse or that we all have to work in Siberia." Otto was learning Spanish and told Warns, "I intend to have Argentina for my first destination."[228]

On 29 January, 1948 Mathilde Kaiser wrote to tell Warns that "today your Christmas parcel . . . arrived here. Hardly can you imagine our indescribable joy, when we packed it out. We had a second Christmas today. We all thank you heartedly for your friendly gifts. May God bless you and your family and help us soon to be in a position to make it good." With deeply expressed gratitude, Mathilde wrote:

> How much your parcel with lard, butter, beef, chicken and its many sweets and substantial food will help us in the next weeks, (which will bring us a height in the nourishment crisis) you will understand when I tell you that we get 40 grams (1 pound=500 grams) of lard per person in the last 4 weeks. For the coming six weeks we only shall get 100 grams of fat and this week we get neither fat nor meat. We 4 persons get for this week 1 pound of noodles, ½ pound soup powder of worst quality. 20 pounds bread, 16 pounds potatoes and 2 pounds fish. And now ask your wife whether she could feed with that your Marian, Kenneth, Marvin and herself for a week.[229]

Mathilde graphically described the toll that a low-calorie diet takes on the human body:

> The want of fat and fresh vegetables (vitamins) causes an everlasting hungry feeling and bad indigestions, during the night nightmares and dreams of good meals. Surely you will imagine, that by such poor nourishment the ability to work (mentally as well as bodily) slackens. We all, thank God, belong to those happy ones who muddle through and in spite of hunger and bad shoes make nice excursions to keep healthy body and mind and by that to escape an infection of T. B.[230]

She was worried about her husband who was currently residing in Koblenz, which was in the French zone of Germany, where "food rations are less than here and I worry about him as he has no one to take care for him. He was the young man you remember. He played piano with one of your comrades for your party 1919."[231]

Soon, the Kaiser family was once again the recipient of Warns' generosity when a second parcel arrived on 14 February, 1948. Mathilde remarked that "we, Lilo [her daughter] and I nearly leapt for joy when all the wonderful things we had missed for so long stood on the table." To create an element of surprise "we built a motley tower of tins and boxes in the sleeping room and waited for the boys." Upon discovering the "motley tower" the boys "came laughing and leaping for joy into the kitchen: That is wonderful. Now we have not to worry about the coming weeks. We all thank you very, very much for your kind gifts dear friend. You can be sure you have helped a family in misery and we can go to meet the next weeks with less sorrow."[232]

Beginning in June of 1948, the Soviet Union attempted to use the Berlin Blockade to isolate the city of Berlin, a city that was divided into Western and Eastern sectors and was located in the Soviet sphere of a divided Germany. United States President Harry Truman, with support from other allies, immediately countered the Berlin Blockade with what became known as the Berlin Airlift.[233] By late 1948, the success of the Berlin Airlift had lifted the spirits of the Kaiser family. Mathilde noted that "finally we are allowed to write via airmail." She happily reported that "since I last wrote you, conditions here turned better. With our new D=Marks we can buy a few things we have been missing for many years. Though we are still kept short, we feel no longer ill, tired and hungry, as we have enough potatoes and vegetables. In the last month we could buy clothing and shoes for our boys." Mathilde explained to John that her daughter, Lilo, was to be married on 8 January, 1949. The hope was that her fiancé Klaus' mother and sister would be able to attend, but then Mathilde explained how Cold War tensions might intervene:

> but as they are living in Berlin it is vague. Conditions
> at Berlin are bad and we send them fruits and potatoes.
> Both are assistants in a hospital of the Russian zone and

it is possible that they can no longer work there, as they are not willing to join Communists Party. We told them to come here to the western zone but they answered that Berlin is standing for Europe and everyone is to stay there. We all hope, and you and your wife will do the same, that America can prevent World War III. With great interest we observed the elections of your president and hope, that Truman is the right man. Or what do you think?[234]

She wondered "whether you got our letters. Above all I hope, that your ailments did not come back again, that you are in best health and that you have been successful in your commercial gardening and in trapping muskrats."[235]

Warns' exposure to gas in July of 1918 resulted in life-long health problems which were aggravated by exposure to the chemicals used in the publishing of the *Wentworth Progress*. His health began to fail in the late 1930s, and lung problems contributed to his untimely death at the Veteran's Administration hospital in Sioux Falls, South Dakota on 2 August, 1952 at the age of fifty-seven.

After the war Anna Warns wrote articles for John's newspaper, *Wentworth Progress,* and worked at Zimmerman's Grocery Store in Wentworth. In 1921 she married William Schoenefeld and they had five children. They farmed in the Wentworth, South Dakota and the Pipestone, Minnesota and Elkton, Clear Lake and Altamont areas of South Dakota.[236] In 1956 they moved to Watertown, South Dakota. In a 1980 article published in the *Watertown Public Opinion,* she was congratulated as the winner of the 106th "Picture of the Week." She had submitted a 1918 photo depicting herself and her mail-delivery horse and buggy. Anne commented:

This snapshot was taken during World War I. My older brother John Warns, now deceased, of Wentworth, Lake Co., S.D. was substitute mail carrier at the time he was drafted into the Army. At that time a soldier's job wasn't held open for him as in WW II, so one day the postmistress, Mrs. Jessie Gerrits, came to see my parents and suggested they let me take my brother's job so it would still be available when my brother returned. So I ended up probably being one of the first and youngest female substitute mail carriers in South Dakota. At that time Wentworth had three routes and each carrier had 15 days' vacation plus some extra days, and I carried for all three. I bought the ponies and buggy for $75 from a pastor since my brother had sold his... In the snapshot are a younger sister, Dorothea Warns, now of Sioux Falls; my mother (Dora), Mrs. Peter Warns; and my younger brother Walter Warns, both now deceased. The mail routes were about 35 miles each and it was usually 4:30 or later before I got back. Now Wentworth has only one route, but more miles. When my brother got back, he decided he didn't want the job of substitute mail carrier anymore. I later sold the ponies and buggy, but I had a lot of fun and enjoyed the experience.[237]

"Dorothea, Dora and Walter Warns pictured with the horse and buggy Anna Warns used to deliver the mail."

Anna Warns died in February, 1994 at the age of ninety-three.

According to his son Marvin, while John Warns did not say much about the war, "he would sometimes share all the items he had collected from the war with his children." On rare occasions "he talked about some of his experiences in the trenches, the fighting and the shooting and shells flying both ways all the time, the terrible conditions of the trenches when it rained, and he talked about the large rats that were in the trenches, and he stated that sometimes when they were without food they would even butcher and eat the rat meat. There were several occasions when they did that."[238] At a family gathering, as Warns was showing his WW I correspondence and memorabilia to his children, they failed to demonstrate what he thought was proper respect. This prompted Warns to write a note that he attached to the bundle of correspondence: "private, not for public viewing."[239] In 2003 the author met with Warns' son Marvin and daughter-in-law Leona in Aberdeen, South Dakota. They agreed to allow access to the vast amount of WW I materials they had accumulated and preserved. In 2005 Marvin Warns was confident that "if Dad were alive today he would approve of the use of his story."[240]

The wartime correspondence to and from Private John Warns provides us with a glimpse of the extent to which even rural South Dakota was enmeshed in the events surrounding the long, destructive and indecisive war that became known as World War One. United States entry into World War One not only ended America's isolationist policies and projected the United States toward global hegemony, it also transformed the lives of this South Dakota family. On the home front the family prayed, wrote letters, assumed new job responsibilities, was exposed to war-time propaganda, and clearly missed John. The community of Wentworth, inspired by official government propaganda, overwhelmingly supported the war effort, acquiescing to the "intolerance as a virtue" culture generated by Wilson's Committee of Public Information. The harsh treatment of the small minority of Wentworth area residents that displayed ambivalence toward the war effort, or attempted to join the Nonpartisan League, represents a short, but regrettable chapter in the community's history. Ironically, it was Woodrow Wilson himself who foresaw how much damage the emotionally charged atmosphere of war could inflict on the country: "Once lead this people into war," Wilson ruminated, "and they'll forget there ever was such a thing as tolerance . . . The spirit of ruthless brutality will enter into the very fibre of our national life, infecting Congress, the courts, the policeman on the beat, the man in the street." Wilson worried that the government itself would not survive: "a nation can't put its strength into a war and keep its head level; it has never been done."[241]

At the state level the repressive policies implemented by the South Dakota Council of Defense were forcefully critiqued by Herbert Schell, who rarely interjected his own views or opinions in his *History of South Dakota*. Schell's assessment of the Council could not have been made more clearly: "The evils resulting from wartime hysteria were not peculiar to South Dakota. Although the State Council cannot be held officially accountable for all the excesses committed in the name of patriotism, the Council's illiberal course of action in matters involving freedom of speech and personal liberty tended to promote a spirit of intolerance which made a mockery of the very principles the nation was seeking to preserve."[242]

As the tumultuous events surrounding World War One unfolded, John Warns' American friend Gil went to Europe and fought with Germany. John attended a church in which the worship services were conducted in the German language and his loyalty had been called into question because of his association with the Nonpartisan League. However, when the United States entered the war against Germany in 1917, and John was drafted in 1918, he answered the call. Later in life it appears that John had completed a two-fold odyssey; as a patriotic American he had waged war on the distant Western front and survived to return home to Wentworth. His odyssey of mind and spirit was perhaps even more remarkable; the grandson of German immigrants, so influenced by war-time propaganda that he referred to Germans as "Huns", had gone to war for the United States versus Germany. But twenty years after the war he had gained a sense of reconciliation—expressed by his acts of generosity toward the Mathilda Kaiser family, people he had been conditioned to view as barbaric "Huns" during the war. From the Western Front the letters written by Private Warns reveal that he was a robust young man who enjoyed a glass of fine wine and a smoke. The actual conditions in the trenches were much more horrible than John ever described in his letters. His formula for survival included reliance on a strong Christian faith, and the knowledge that his family members, in particular his mother Dora and his sister Anna, were sustaining him with their prayers and keeping him connected to the home front with their letters and, of course, some Velvet pipe tobacco. The horrifying experience of trench warfare in World War I had a way of driving men back to the basics of who they were and what they believed.

ENDNOTES

1 David Fromkin, *Europe's Last Summer: Who Started The Great War In 1914?* (New York: Random House, Inc., 2004), p. 121 and pp. 132-136. Fromkin observed that the lack of security surrounding the Archduke's visit was alarming, given that in the twenty years of Princip's life, twenty heads of state had been assassinated, including William McKinley, President of the United States, in 1901.

2 Since 1900 twelve million immigrants had arrived in America. David M. Kennedy, *Over Here: The First World War and American Society* (New York: Oxford University Press, 2004), p. 11.

3 Thomas Fleming, *The Illusion of Victory: America In World War One,* (New York: Basic Books, 2003), pp. 60-61.

4 *Wentworth, South Dakota Centennial History, 1881-1981, p. 17*

5 *Wentworth, South Dakota Centennial History, 1881-1981,* p. 23.

6 *Wentworth, South Dakota Centennial History, 1881-1981,* p. 26.

7 Leona Warns Letter to Richard Lofthus, 30 November, 2005.

8 Indiana University history professor Samuel B. Harding developed a war study plan for high school students that was distributed to nearly 800,000 secondary school teachers and students. It referred to the Germans as bestial Huns. David Kennedy, *Over Here: The First World War and American Society,* p. 56.

9 The original copies of the war-time correspondence of the Warns family are in the possession of Paula Scholten, Inwood, Iowa, grand-daughter of John Warns.

10 Marvin Warns Letter to Richard Lofthus, 1 June, 2005.

11 Gil to John Warns, 29 March, 1915. Gil's graphic account of the skirmishes along the Yser River in late October and early November of 1914 included a hand-crafted map of the battle. Gil's version matches references to these skirmishes found in secondary sources such as S. L. A. Marshall, *World War I* (New York: Houghton Mifflin Company, 2001), pp. 132-133. The confrontations that Gil is describing took place just prior to the First Battle of Ypres in 1914.

12 Ibid., p. 2.

13 Ibid., p. 2.

14 Ibid., p. 4.

15 Ibid., p. 4.

16 Ibid., pp. 10-11.

17 Ibid., pp. 12-14.

18 Ibid., p. 18.

19 John Keegan, *The First World War* (New York: Alfred K. Knopf, 1999), p. 135.

20 Richard Harding Davis, *With The Allies* (New York, 1 December, 1914).

21 Edith Wharton as quoted in the American Experience documentary entitled *The Great War: Episode One* (WGBH Educational Foundation, 2017).

22 Gil to John Warns, 29 March, 1915. Gil's last name remains a mystery as he did not include it in this letter written from 613 First St., Grand Forks, North Dakota.

23 Gil to John Warns, 29 March, 1915.

Chapter Two

24 Keegan, The First World War, p. 265.

25 Martin Gilbert, *The First World War: A Complete History* (New York: Henry Holt and Company, 1994) p. 308.

26 *The War Message and Facts Behind It,* War Information Series, No. 1 (Committee On Public Information, Washington, D. C., June 1917), p. 15.

27 Ibid., p. 18

28 Fleming, *The Illusion of Victory,* p. 26.

29 *The War Message and Facts Behind It,* War Information Series, No. 1, p. 22.

30 Ibid. p. 23

31 A. Scott Berg, as quoted in the American Experience documentary, *The Great War: Episode One,* written and directed by Stephen Ives, produced by Amanda Pollak (WGBH, Educational Foundation, 2017).

32 Kennedy, *Over Here: The First World War and American Society,* p. 51.

33 Ibid., pp. 33-41.

34 Ibid., p. 4.

35 Fleming, *The Illusion of Victory: America In World War I,* p 118.

36 Ibid., p. 94.

37 Farmer, Degler and De Santis, *Introduction to American History, Volume II, Since 1865* (Redding, California: BVT Publishing, 2011), pp. 345-346.

38 A Scott Berg, *Wilson,* (New York: G. P. Putnam's Sons, 2013), p. 497.

39 Ibid., pp. 496-497.

40 *Wentworth Enterprise,* April 12, 1917. This letter was originally published in the *Sioux City Journal,* 5 April, 1917.

41 Herbert S. Schell, *History of South Dakota* (Pierre: South Dakota State Historical Society Press, 2004), p. 270.

42 Schell, *History of South Dakota*, p. 271.

43 Schell, *History of South Dakota*, p. 273. Similar legislation was passed in Iowa and David Kennedy refers to this type of legislation as the product of a "blameless fury that knew few restraints." Kennedy, *Over Here: The First World War and American Society*, p. 68.

44 Kennedy, *Over Here: The First World War and American Society*, p. 68.

45 Ida Rottluf to John Warns, 25 October, 1917. This letter may indicate that Ida and John held differing opinions on the war at this point, but her statement: "we don't agree"; could also refer to her own disagreement with other German Americans who were still supporting Germany. The letter does clearly refer to John's impending entry into the military. There is no other documentary or anecdotal evidence that Ida and John disagreed on the war at this point. Ten years later, on July 10, 1927 Ida Rottluf and John Warns were married.

46 Michael J. Lansing, *Insurgent Democracy: The Nonpartisan League in North American Politics* (Chicago and London: The University of Chicago Press, 2015), p. 19.

47 Ibid., p. 39

48 Warns' actual certificate of membership is in the possession of his grand-daughter, Paula Scholten of Inwood, Iowa. Following the war John Warns joined the National Nonpartisan League on 15 July, 1919.

49 Gilbert Fite, *Peter Norbeck: Prairie Statesman* (Columbia: University of Missouri Press, 1948), p. 62.

50 Lansing, *Insurgent Democracy: The Nonpartisan League in North American Politics*, p. 104.

51 Theodore Roosevelt, "The Ghost Dance of the Shadow Huns," October 1, 1917 in *Roosevelt in the Kansas City Star: War-Time Editorials* (New York: Houghton Mifflin, 1921), pp. 5-8.

52 Theodore Roosevelt, "Anti-Bolshevism", June 5, 1918, p. 158, "Murder, Treason and Parlor Anarchy", July 18, 1918, p. 182, "Spies and Slackers", September 24, 1918, p. 223, "Good Luck To The Anti-Bolshevists, September 12, 1918, pp. 213-215, in *Roosevelt in the Kansas City Star: War-Time Editorials* (New York: Houghton Mifflin, 1921).

53 *Wentworth Enterprise*, 17 January, 1918.

54 *Wentworth Enterprise*, 7 February, 1918.

55 *Wentworth Enterprise*, 7 February, 1918.

56 *Wentworth Enterprise*, 7 February, 1918.

57 Norbeck to Sheriff E. H. Keller, 4 February, 1918 as quoted by Gilbert Fite in *Peter Norbeck: Prairie Statesman*, p. 65.

58 Ibid.

59 Lansing, *Insurgent Democracy: The Nonpartisan League in North American Politics*, p. 109.

60 Gilbert Fite, *Peter Norbeck: Prairie Statesman*, pp. 65-66.

61 Curt Brown, *Minnesota 1918: When Flu, Fire, and War Ravaged the State* (Saint Paul: Minnesota State Historical Society Press, 2018), pp. 73-75.

62 Ibid., p. 81.

63 Lansing, *Insurgent Democracy: The Nonpartisan League in North American Politics,* pp. 120-124.

64 Irene Thompson to Dear friend, 14 March, 1918.

65 Irene Thompson to Dear friend, 25 March, 1918. Irene told John that she was a teacher with thirty-seven pupils. She wrote "I live at Richville (Minnesota) a little town on the Soo."

66 South Dakota, *Legislative Manual* (1919), p. 442, Fite, *Peter Norbeck*, pp. 76-68, The *Wentworth Enterprise* commented on the elections of 1918 with the following: "Considerable interest was injected into the campaign this year because of the attempt of famous Nonpartisan League to gain control of the state's law making machinery. Unofficial results show that they were given a severe beating and failed to win a state or federal office." *Wentworth Enterprise*, November 7, 1918.

67 Frederick Lewis Allen, *Only Yesterday: An Informal History of the 1920s* (New York and London: Harper & Brothers Publishers, 1931), pp. 58-59.

68 Robert K. Murray, *Red Scare: A Study In National Hysteria, 1919-1920* (Minneapolis: University of Minnesota Press, 1955), p. 84.

Chapter Three

69 Order of Induction into Military Service of the United States, Form 1028, located in the Warns Family Papers.

70 Individual Pay Record Book, located in the Warns Family Papers.

71 Farmer, Degler and De Santis, *Introduction to American History, Volume II, Since 1865,* p. 339.

72 Keystone View Company Stereograph, Number 58. The California Museum of Photography at the University of California, Riverside has the original negatives for all the stereographs produced by the Keystone View Company. The "Selective Service Law of 1917 required all males between the ages of 21 and 31 to register for National Army Service." See C. J. Masseck, *Official Brief History 89th Division, U. S. A., 1917-1918-1919* (no publication date available), p. 1.

73 Keystone View Company, Stereograph Number 60. The term "doughboys" apparently derived from the nickname "dobies," which had been given to infantry troops in Texas who were often covered with the dust of the "adobe" soils found along the Rio Grande. Lawrence Stallings, *The Doughboys: The Story of the AEF, 1917-1918 (New York: Harper and Row, 1963),* p. 5.

74 Keystone View Company, Stereograph Number 60.

75 Ibid., Stereograph Number 71.

76 Ibid., Stereograph Number 67.

77 Ibid., Stereograph Number 64.

78 Keystone View Company Stereograph, Number 77.

79 John Warns to Anna Warns, May, 1918.

80 John Warns was now one of approximately thirty-five thousand South Dakotans who served in World War I, according to Joseph Mills Hanson, see *South Dakota in the World War, 1917-1919* (Pierre: South Dakota State Historical Society Press, 1940), p. iv. Hanson, a Yankton, South Dakota author, was also a World War I veteran.

81 Laurence Stallings, *The Doughboys*, p. 348.

82 John Warns to Anna Warns, May 1918.

83 John Warns to Mother and all, 1 May, 1918. John's mother Dora was forty-six years old in 1918.

84 John Warns to Anna Warns, May, 1918.

85 John Warns to folks, May, 1918.

86 C. J. Masseck, *Official Brief History 89ᵗʰ Division, U. S. A., 1917-1918-1919* (no publication dated available), p. 2.

87 Hanson, *South Dakota In The World War, 1917-1919*, p. 347

88 John Warns to Anna Warns, May 1918. The diet and training received in places like Camp Funston often improved the health of the recruits.

89 John Warns to Anna Warns, May, 1918.

90 John Warns to Mother, 27 May, 1918.

91 John Warns to folks, 28 May, 1918.

92 Hanson, *South Dakota in the World War, 1917-1919*, p. 351. Between April and October of 1918, 1.6 million American soldiers were shipped to Europe, see David Laskin, *The Long Way Home: An American Journey from Ellis Island to the Great War*, (New York: Harper Perennial, 2010), p. 189.

93 John Warns to Mother, Dad and all, 31 May, 1918. John's father, Peter, was fifty years old in 1918.

94 *Wentworth Enterprise*, April 25, 1918.

95 *Wentworth Enterprise*, May 2, 1918.

96 John Warns to Anna Warns, May, 1918.

97 *Wentworth Enterprise*, June 4, 1918.

98 John Warns to Anna Warns, 1 June, 1918.

99 *Wentworth, South Dakota Centennial History, 1881-1981* (Wentworth, South Dakota: Wentworth Historical Committee, 1981), p. 68. General John Pershing had also sailed to Europe on the Baltic in May, 1917, see Fleming, *Illusions of Victory: America in World War I*, p. 105.

100 John Warns to Mother, no date. In this letter Private Warns claims that he is not the least bit seasick, indicating that it was written in route to England early June, 1918.

101 John Warns to Dear Mother and all, no date available, the reference to U-boats places this letter in early June, 1918, onboard The Baltic.

102 *Wentworth, South Dakota Centennial History, 1881-1981,* p. 68.

103 John Warns to Mother, no date. The reference to mothers who have lost everything seems to indicate that this letter was written from Europe, probably in June of 1918.

104 John Warns to Anna Warns, 17 June, 1918.

105 John Warns to Dear Mother and All, 21 June, 1918. This letter was published in a newspaper and is in the Warns Family Papers, the name of the newspaper is not available, although later in 1918 John Warns mentions in a letter to his family that some of his letters had been published in the *Sioux Falls Argus Leader* and the *Sioux City Journal*.

Chapter Four

106 American Experience documentary, *The Great War: Episode Two,* produced and direct by Amanda Pollak, written by Stephen Ives (WGBH, Educational Foundation, 2017).

107 Martin Gilbert, *The First World War: A Complete History* (New York: Henry Holt and Company, 1994), p. 421.

108 Ibid., Stallings, *Doughboys,* p. 203.

109 Hanson, *South Dakota In The World War, 1917-1919,* p. 356.

110 John Warns to Anna Warns, 9 July, 1918.

111 *Wentworth Enterprise,* November 1, 1917 and November 15, 1917.

112 Kennedy, *Over Here: The First World War and American Society,* p. 62. The photodrama, *"The Kaiser, The Beast of Berlin,* was shown in the Wentworth Opera House on October 13, 1918. Admission was twenty-five cents for children and fifty cents for adults, Wentworth, *Wentworth Enterprise,* October 13, 1918.

113 *Over the Top* was a silent movie, made in 1918 and directed by Wilfrid North. It appears that no copies of this movie have survived. The expression "over the top" was used to refer to the act of charging out of a trench to engage the enemy in combat.

114 Anna Warns to Dearest Brother, 25 June 1918. Anna (nicknamed "Tommy" or "Tom") was eighteen years old in 1918. John Warns was twenty-three years old in 1918. He came from a family that included six other siblings. John was the oldest, and in 1918 the children included Martha, twenty-two, Martin, twenty-two, Anna, eighteen, Walter, fifteen, Dorothea (nicknamed "Dimples"), twelve, and Selma (Sally) nine. At a reunion of the Warns family in Madison, South Dakota, 11 September, 2004 the author was privileged to meet Selma, the

last surviving member of John Warns' immediate family. Selma was ninety-four in 2004. Anna's friend Agnes, mentioned in this letter, was Agnes Oberheu, daughter of Pastor Ferinand Oberheu of Saint Peter's Lutheran Church in Wentworth.

115 In an interview with the author in 2005, John's son Marvin explained that Anna bought the horse and buggy from Pastor Ferinand Oberheu for $75.

116 Anna Warns to John Warns, 1 July, 1918.

117 John Warns to Dear Tommy, 12 July 1918.

118 John Warns to Anna Warns, 13 July, 1918.

119 John Warns to Dear Mother, 6 August, 1918.

120 Hanson, *South Dakota in the World War,* pp. 361-363. Three types of gas were used during World War I. Chlorine could destroy bronchial tubes and lungs. Phosgene was more powerful than Chlorine, it was invisible and in fatal doses it could cause a drowning spasm that might last for forty-eight hours. Mustard gas often caused headaches and pneumonia, it smelled like onions or garlic, and "in more severe exposures men might cough up a cast of their mucous membranes, lose their genitals or be burnt right through to the bone." Denis Winter, *Death's Men: Soldiers of the Great War,* (London, England: Penguin Books, 1978), pp. 121-123. In an interview with the author in 2005, John's son Marvin explained that his father John had been exposed to mustard gas.

121 John Warns to Dear Tommy, 13 December, 1918.

122 John Warns to Dear Mother and all, 2 September, 1918. Uncle Paul was a brother to John's father Peter Warns.

123 Hanson, *South Dakota In The World War, 1917-1919,* p. 362.

124 C. J. Masseck, *Official Brief History 89th Division, U. S. A., 1917-1918-1919* (no publication date available), p. 11.

125 Hanson, *South Dakota In The World War, 1917-1919,* p. 367.

126 John Warns to Mother, 21 July, 1918. The "big drive" that Warns is referring to is the build-up to the Saint Mihiel Offensive of September 12, 1918.

127 John Warns to Mother, 10 August, 1918. Private Warns mentions that he dropped a packet with many letters while marching and was not able to stop and pick it up. This explains why many letters to him have not survived. "Tanglefoot" was the trade name for a sticky substance made of rosin and castor oil and used to catch flies. It also was a slang term for whiskey.

128 John Warns to Anna Warns, 11 August, 1918.

129 John Warns to Folks, 18 August, 1918. Pierre Weiss was the son of C. H. Weiss, a pioneer merchant of Wentworth. The encounter between John Warns and Pierre Weiss in the French hospital was the subject of an article entitled "Wentworth Boys Meet in France", dated 15 August, 1918 in the *Wentworth Enterprise.* Weiss reported that he had a shrapnel wound in his foot, and that Warns was hospitalized because of a case of mumps. While Warns may well have had a

case of the mumps, he was also in the hospital because he had been exposed to poisonous gas.

130 John Warns to Mother and all, 22 August, 1918. The term "Fritz" was a slang word used to refer to the Germans.

131 John Warns to Mother, 29 August and 9 September, 1918.

132 Jake Warns to John Warns, 11 September, 1918.

133 Edward Coffman, *The War To End All Wars, The American Military Experience In World War I* (New York: Oxford University Press, 1968), p. 277

134 Ibid., p. 278.

135 "September 10, 1918! Memories of the St, Mihiel Drive Kept Alive by 355th Reunion Opening Here today", *Hastings Daily Tribune,* 10 September, 1938.

136 Joseph Mills Hanson, p. 381.

137 Joseph Mills Hanson, p. 388.

138 "September 10, 1918! Memories of the St, Mihiel Drive Kept Alive by 355th Reunion Opening Here today", *Hastings Daily Tribune,* 10 September, 1938.

139 Joseph Mills Hanson, pp. 390-391.

140 Edward Coffman, *The War To End All Wars*, p. 283.

141 C. J. Masseck, *Official Brief History 89th Division, U. S. A., 1917-1918-1919*, pp. 18-19.

142 John Warns to folks, 26 September, 1918. In his book entitled *The Doughboys: American And The First World War* (New York: The Overlook Press, 2000), p. 265 Garry Mead points out that soldiers sometimes turned to smoking to cover the smell of rotting corpses.

143 John Warns to Dear Tommy, 13 December, 1918.

144 Joseph Mills Hanson, p. 397.

145 John Warns to Mother and all, 3 October, 1918.

146 Edward Coffman, *The War To End All Wars,* p. 303.

147 John S. D. Eisenhower, *Yanks: The Epic Story of the American Army in World War I,* (New York: The Free Press, 2001), p. 198-199.

148 C. J. Masseck, *Official Brief History 89th Division, U. S. A., 1917-1918-1919,* p. 21.

149 Ida Rottluf to John Warns, 21 October, 1918.

150 John Warns to Dearest Dimples, 23 October, 1918.

151 John Warns to Dearest Mother and All, 17 October, 1918.

152 John Warns to Mother and all, 3 October, 1918 and 17 October, 1918.

153 Pastor F. Oberheu to John Warns, 16 October, 1918.

154 Ibid., In a phone interview on 10 September, 2003, Marvin Warns pointed out that his father John shared the contents of this letter with him as he was sent to fight in the Korean War. Marvin Warns remarked, "When I went to Korea, just before I left, Dad took me over to his trunk and he pulled out that letter and he said just read through this Marvin, this is what I think it is all about."

Pastor Ferinand Oberheu served as the pastor at Saint Peters Lutheran Church in Wentworth for forty-five years (1895-1940). During those years he also taught parochial school for twenty-three years, as reported in *Wentworth, South Dakota Centennial History, 1881-1981*, p. 13.

155 Edward Coffman, p. 345

156 Ibid., p. 346.

157 Joseph Mills Hanson, p. 420.

158 C. J. Masseck, *Official Brief History 89th Division, U. S. A., 1917-1918-1919*, p. 39.

159 Jake Warns to John Warns, 10 November, 1918.

160 Burr Price, *Special Telegram To The Herald*. This is from a photocopy of Price's telegram found in the Warns Family Papers. The newspaper is identified only as the "Herald" and no date is provided. Price entered Stenay, France at almost exactly the same time as Private Warns.

161 Captain Eddie Rickenbacker as quoted in Andrew Carroll's, *My Fellow Soldiers: General John Pershing and the Americans Who Helped Win the Great War* (New York, Penguin Press, 2017), pp. 315-316.

162 John Warns hand-written note found in the Warns Family Papers.

163 Burr Price, *Special Telegram to the Herald.*

164 Cousin Hattie to Dear Cousin, 17 December, 1918. Hattie also told John "they are still fighting the "flu" here in Frisco, they don't wear the masks anymore tho."

165 *Wentworth Enterprise*, November 14, 1918.

166 Selma Warns to John Warns, 29 November, 1918.

167 John Warns to Mother, 15 November, 1918.

168 John Warns to Mother, no date. Because Private Warns describes crossing the Meuse River, this letter was written shortly after November 11, 1918. S and S is a reference to the publication Stars and Stripes.

169 Laurence Stallings, The Doughboys, pp. 376-377. In an Appendix Stallings compiled the statistics for each US Division's involvement in World War I.

170 Masseck, *Official Brief History 89th Division, U. S. A., 1917-1918-1919*, pp. 40-41.

Chapter Five

171 Masseck, *Official Brief History 89th Division, U. S. A., 1917-1918-1919*, p. 42.

172 Joseph Mills Hanson, *South Dakota In The World War, 1917-1919*, pp. 428-435.

173 John Warns to folks, 26 November, 1918.

174 Jake Warns to John Warns, 10 October, 1918.

175 John Warns to Dad, 26 November, 1918. The Wilson administration created the Committee on Public Information as its official government propaganda

agency, and it became, in the words of David Kennedy, a "crude propaganda mill." The CPI hired "Four-Minute Men" who gave short speeches in support of the war effort. In 1918 the Four-Minute Men "were specifically encouraged to use atrocity stories." David Kennedy, *Over Here: The First World War and American Society,* pp. 59-62.

176 Masseck, *Official Brief History 89th Division, U. S. A., 1917-1918-1919,* p. 43.

177 John Warns to Dear folks, uncles, aunts, cousins and all, 23 December, 1918. This letter has survived in a typed format and was published in a newspaper, the name of which is unknown.

178 Ibid.

179 Compounding the tragedy of war was the Spanish influenza pandemic that swept the globe in 1918-1919, killing approximately 675,000 Americans in 1918 alone. Wentworth is located in Lake County and in 1918 there were twenty-one reported influenza deaths in Lake County. Lawrence County reported the highest number of influenza deaths in South Dakota, one-hundred and forty-five. *Division of Vital Statistics, Thirteenth Annual Report, December 31, 1918.* As quoted at www.sdhistory.org/arc/1918deaths.htm.

180 Anna Warns to John Warns, 25 December, 1918.

181 Anna Warns to John Warns, 13 January and 4 April, 1919.

182 John Warns to Dear Anna. No date available. The reference to receiving a Christmas packet would date this letter sometime in January, 1919.

183 Uncle Jake to Dear John, 6 January, 1919.

184 John Warns to Dear Mother and All, 4 January, 1919.

185 Uncle Jake to John Warns, 27 February, 1919.

186 John Warns to Dearest Tommy, 22 January, 1919.

187 Anna Warns to Dear Johnny Boy, 18 January, 1918. "Over There" was written by George M. Cohan in 1917, https://www.google.com/#safe=off&q=over+th ere+world+war+i+song, accessed 3 August, 2016. "I May Be Gone for a Long Long Time" was written by Lew Brown in 1917, https://www.google.com/#sa fe=off&q=over+there+world+war+i+song, accessed 3 August, 2016. "Dimples" was a nickname for John and Anna's sister, Dorothea Warns.

188 John Warns to Anna Warns, 1 February, 1919.

189 Cousin Hattie to Dear Cousin John, 19 February, 1919.

190 John Warns, *Pocket Diary,* 1918-1919, p. 2.

191 *Pocket Diary,* p. 4.

192 https://en.wikipedia.org/wiki/Georges_Clemenceau, accessed 24 July, 2018.

193 John Warns to Anna Warns, 19 February 1919.

194 John Warns to Anna Warns, 2 March, 1919. The original copy of this letter was dated 1918 by John Warns, but that appears to be a mistake as the contents of the letter clearly indicate that John is writing from inside Germany. "Shell Shock" was a term used during World War One to refer to a variety of psychological

disturbances which afflicted soldiers after combat experience. It would later be referred to as "Battle Fatigue" and subsequently diagnosed as Post Traumatic Stress Disorder (PTSD).

195 Ibid.

196 John Warns to Anna Warns, 4 March, 1918.

197 Ibid.

198 Warns to Mother, Dad and All, 22 September, 1918.

199 Nicholas V. Riasanovsky, *A History of Russia*, (New York: Oxford University Press, 1993) p. 477.

200 John Warns to Anna Warns, 4 March, 1919.

201 *Pocket Diary*, pp. 9-10.

202 John Warns to Anna Warns, 11 March, 1919.

203 John Warns to Anna Warns, 2 April, 1919.

204 The Virginia Dare winery originated in North Carolina. https://www.virginiadarewinery.com/, accessed 18 July, 2016.

205 John Warns to Anna, 7 April, 1919.

206 Ibid.

207 Ibid.

208 Ibid.

209 Ibid.

210 John Warns to Anna, 19 April, 1919.

211 Ibid.

212 John Warns to Tommy and all, 24 April, 1919.

213 *Pocket Diary*, p. 15.

214 John Warns to Mother, 11 May, 1919.

215 *Pocket Diary*, pp. 16-18.

216 *New York Times,* 24 May, 1919, 25 May, 1919.

217 John Warns to Tommy, 25 May, 1919.

218 *Pocket Diary*, p. 19.

Chapter Six

219 In a 2005 interview with John's son Marvin, the author was informed that as a teenager, on Monday mornings, John Warns would take the news from Pastor Oberheu of Saint Peter's Lutheran Church to the Wentworth Enterprise newspaper. John also swept the floors, folded papers and was writing articles for the newspaper at the age of fifteen-sixteen.

220 Marvin Warns, *1995 Lake Country History*, p. 848.

221 "Wentworth Man Compiles History of Lake County", *Madison Daily Leader*, 16 February, 1954.

222 Marvin and Leona Warns to Richard Lofthus, 3 January, 2004.

223 Mathilde Kaiser to Dear friend John, 7 January, 1948.

224 Mathilde Kaiser to Dear friend John, 24 January, 1948.

225 Ibid.

226 Ibid.

227 Ibid.

228 Otto Kaiser to Dear Sir, 8 January, 1948.

229 Mathilde Kaiser to Dear friend John, 29 January, 1948.

230 Ibid.

231 Ibid.

232 Mathilde Kaiser to Dear friend John, 19 February, 1948.

233 https://en.wikipedia.org/wiki/Berlin_Blockade, accessed 24 July, 2018.

234 Mathilde Kaiser to Dear Friend John, 15 November, 1948.

235 Ibid.

236 Phone interview with Arla Elverud, 17 April, 2014. At the time of the interview Arla, the youngest daughter of Anna Warns, was living in Cornelius, Oregon.

237 "Memories of a Former Kid", *Watertown Public Opinion,* 14 March, 1980.

238 Interview with Marvin Warns, Aberdeen, South Dakota, 10 September, 2003.

239 Interview with Marvin Warns, 2005.

240 Ibid.

241 Richard Striner, *Woodrow Wilson and World War I: A Burden Too Great to Bear* (Lanhan, MD: Rowan and Littlefield Publishers, 2014), p. 103, as quoted in *1917: Lenin, Wilson, And the Birth Of The New World Disorder* by Arthur Herman, pp. 151-152.

242 Herbert Schell, *History of South Dakota,* p. 273.

BIBLIOGRAPHY

Allen, Frederick Lewis. *Only Yesterday: An Informal History of the 1920s.* New York and London: Harper and Brothers Publishers, 1931.

Berg, A. Scott. *Wilson.* New York: G. P. Putnam's Sons, 2013.

Brown, Curt. *Minnesota 1918: When Flu, Fire, and War Ravaged the State.* Saint Paul: Minnesota Historical Society Press, 2018.

Carroll, Andrew. *My Fellow Soldiers: General John Pershing and the Americans Who Helped Win the Great War.* New York: Penguin Press, 2017.

Coffman, Edward. *The War To End All Wars, The American Military Experience In World War I.* New York: Oxford University Press, 1968.

Davis, Richard Harding. *With The Allies.* New York, 1 December, 1914.

Eisenhower, John S. D. *Yanks: The Epic Story of the American Army in World War I.* New York: The Free Press, 2001.

Fleming, Thomas. *The Illusion of Victory, America In World War I.* New York: Basic Books, 2003.

Fromkin, David. *Europe's Last Summer: Who Started The Great War in 1914?* New York: Random House, Inc., 2004.

Farmer, Degler and De Santis, *Introduction to American History, Volume II, Since 1865.* Redding, California: BVT Publishing, 2011.

Fite, Gilbert. *Peter Norbeck: Prairie Statesman.* Columbia, Missouri: University of Missouri Press, 1948.

Gilbert, Martin. *The First World War: A Complete History.* New York: Henry Holt and Company, 1994.

Hanson, Joseph Mills. *South Dakota in the World War, 1917-1919.* Pierre, South Dakota: South Dakota Historical Society Press, 1940.

Herman, Arthur. *1917: Lenin, Wilson, And The Birth Of The New World Disorder.* New York: HarperCollins Publishers, 2017.

Keegan, John. *The First World War.* New York: Alfred A. Knopf, 1998.

Kennedy, David. *Over Here: The First World War and American Society.* New York: Oxford University Press, 2004

Lansing, Michael. *Insurgent Democracy: The Nonpartisan League in North American Politics.* Chicago and London: The University of Chicago Press, 2015.

Laskin, David. *The Long Way Home: An American Journey from Ellis Island to the Great War.* New York: Harper Perennial, 2010.

Marshall, S. L. A. *World War I.* New York: Houghton Mifflin Company, 2001.

Masseck, C. J. *Official Brief History 89th Division, U S. A., 1917-1918-1919.*

Murray, Robert K. *Red Scare: A Study In National Hysteria, 1919-1920.* Minneapolis: University of Minnesota Press, 1955.

Riasanovsky, Nicholas V. *A History of Russia.* New York: Oxford University Press, 1993.

Roosevelt, Theodore. *Roosevelt in the Kansas City Star: War-Time Editorials.* New York: Houghton Mifflin, 1921.

Schell, Herbert S. *History of South Dakota*. Pierre, South Dakota: South Dakota Historical Society Press, 2004.

Stallings, Laurence. *The Doughboys*. New York: Harper and Row, 1963.

Striner, Richard. *Woodrow Wilson and World War I: A Burden Too Great to Bear*. Landon, Maryland: Roman and Littlefield Publishers, 2014.

Winter, Denis. *Death's Men: Soldiers of the Great War*. London, England: Penguin Books, 1978.

Zieger, Robert. *America's Great War: World War I And The American Experience*. New York: Rowman & Littlefield Publishers, Inc., 2000.

Newspapers:

Hastings Daily Tribune, 1938

Madison Daily Leader, 1954

New York Times, 1919

Watertown Public Opinion, 1980

Wentworth Enterprise, 1917-1918

Documentaries:

The Great War: Episode One. Written and directed by Stephen Ives, produced by Amanda Pollak. WGBH, PBS Educational Foundation, 2017. *Episode Two*. Produced and directed by Amanda Pollak, written by Stephen Ives.

Made in the USA
Monee, IL
24 August 2020